A LIFE LIVED, DESPITE IT ALL

A Memoir

DR. EARL W. HENDRICKS

ISBN 979-8-89043-537-8 (paperback)
ISBN 979-8-89130-804-6 (hardcover)
ISBN 979-8-89043-538-5 (digital)

Christian Faith Publishing
832 Park Avenue
Meadville, PA 16335
www.christianfaithpublishing.com

Printed in the United States of America

Introduction

"WRITE A BOOK!" "Why don't you write a book?" For years now, many people, including my wife, have been encouraging me to write a book. So here I am!

The questions confronting me have always been: Why a book? And what should I write about? Well, what I have come to realize is, why not a book? And like everyone else, don't I have a story to tell?

It might well be that no one will have the slightest bit of interest in what I have to say. But that doesn't mean I shouldn't write! What I write might never get published, and that will be fine too. That still should not stop me from writing. What I write, I write first of all for me. I am sure it is going to be a great therapy to finally put down on paper my thoughts, my experiences, my trials, my victories, the things that I have regretted, and most certainly the things that I am most grateful for.

One thing that had always held me back from starting to write was that I had always wondered what the theme of a book should be. As I have thought about it, it occurred to me that if I waited to develop a theme, I would probably never get started. So why not just get started? Just start writing and let it come. After all, I have been writing all my life: from short stories to newspaper columns to all those papers I had to write while completing a doctoral degree.

One of the things I have been thinking a lot about recently are the various people who have had some significant influence in my life—for good or bad. It is true that no life is ever lived alone, that nothing of value is ever achieved alone. There are always people who have contributed in one way or another to the life you live and I would like to somehow pay homage to some of those people.

Some of them might not mean anything to others, but to me, they are my heroes. As I have lived my life, they are the ones who have helped to shape the person I have become, and for that, I am very grateful.

Now, I am sure that many of them will probably have absolutely no interest in being written about, but like I said, I am writing about what is important to me. Some of these people have passed on, and some are still with us, so I am hoping that I might yet have the chance to say thank you for all that they have been to me. So here I am! I'm writing a book! Here goes!

An Unexpected Turn

It was a warm September day in 1964 when I first met the Meads.

As a ward of the court, it was the responsibility of the government to find boarding for me as I started my high school career at Manning's High School in Savanna-La-Mar, the capital of the parish of Westmoreland in Jamaica.

I had arrived late for orientation, so there was no one on the campus except two ladies whose names I learned were Mrs. Mead and Ms. Duhaney. After we were introduced, the welfare officer and I set out to find the family I was to live with as a boarder while I attended school. When we arrived at the house, for a reason that still eludes me, I refused to get out of the vehicle and was adamant that I did not want to stay there. Maybe it was because I was only twelve years old and this was the first time I was going to be away from all my brothers and sisters, I don't know. But even before I had gone into the house or met the people there, something in me knew this was not the place for me.

What was significant was that I was not a rebellious kid who got into trouble by defying adults or those in authority. Insisting on having my way in opposition to what an adult had decided was not who I was at all. And understand this: this was in the year of our Lord, 1964! Back then, children were supposed to be seen and not heard. As a child, you did as you were told, and that was it. And yet here I was, absolutely determined that I was not going to stay with the people the government had chosen for me to board with.

The welfare officer, unable to understand my reluctance, left me seated in the car and went into the house to meet the people who lived there. I have no idea how long he was in the house, but when he came back, his single statement to me was "You are not staying here." He never explained what he had seen or why he felt that home was not an appropriate home for a twelve-year-old boy. He just got back in the car, started it up, and drove off.

Still not saying anything, he turned the car around and headed back up to the school campus. Again, I have absolutely no idea why he did that. He just did. He didn't say anything to me on the short journey back to the campus; he just drove there as if he was being led to head back there.

When we got to the campus, only Mrs. Mead was still there, and as we drove up, she walked over to the car and inquired if there was a problem. The welfare officer explained that I had refused to stay at the home they had chosen for me to board, and I don't remember him saying anything about his concerns. Mrs. Mead's response was simply "Well then, why doesn't he come and stay with us?"

I promise you that that was the totality of the conversation between the welfare officer and Mrs. Mead before I got my suitcase with my few belongings and followed this lady that I was meeting for the first time back to her house, which was located on the campus grounds.

Not only was I meeting her for the first time, she was a white English lady who was married with seven children of her own. Now there would be eight of us, and at twelve years old, I was the oldest.

I did not and still do not know what the government's policy was regarding placing wards of the court in foster homes, but I am certain the way I ended up living with the Meads could not possibly have been according to policy.

Here was a white family that I had never met before, and I am sure the welfare officer had never met before either, and yet he left me with them and went off about his business. To this day, I have never seen or heard from him again. And yet what he did that day was to prove pivotal in the person I was to become.

The Meads came to Jamaica from England in 1959 with four young children and, by 1964, had added three more kids to the family. In total, the Meads had six boys and one girl. When I came to live with them, the oldest was only ten years old and the youngest was just two. And now they had added a twelve-year-old boy to the family. When Mrs. Mead invited me to come live with them, her husband was not at home. She had made that decision completely on her own. It was only after he returned home that he was told that there had been an addition to the family. I do not know what kind of conversation took place between Mr. and Mrs. Mead in private, but he seemed to accept it as if it was the normal and natural thing to do.

I had never met a white family before, much less had any interaction with one. But when I went with Mrs. Mead that morning, I immediately felt at home. I was not nervous, had no concerns, no sense of apprehension, none of that. For some unexplained reason, I felt as if this was where I belonged even though I was meeting the family for the very first time. I was a little intrigued at first, surrounded by a family of white people, but somehow never felt like I was completely out of place.

So how did I end up here? How did I end up on that high school campus that Saturday morning in September 1964 and find myself being part of a white family I had never seen or met before? Well, that story really began some years before.

Left Behind

I WAS ONE of five children born to my parents who, in 1956, had packed up and left Jamaica for England to seek a better life for themselves. I was the third of five and was only four years old at the time. I had two older brothers and two younger sisters, the youngest of which was only six months old.

We were too young to understand all the ramifications of our parents leaving us and going off to England, but I would presume it was to get themselves settled so that they could send for their kids at a later date. They left all five of us with one of my father's sisters who herself had two kids of her own.

My aunt Vena lived up in the hills of St. Elizabeth in a little town called Balaclava. It was more like a village than a town really, and the people there mostly eked out a living as subsistence farmers if they had a piece of land they could farm. There were no businesses or companies to offer employment to anyone. In fact, as I recall, the only business in the little village was a small grocery store that sold the bare essentials like sugar, flour, cornmeal, soap, and some tin foods.

I do not remember what the size of my aunt's house was, but it could not have been of much size. People living in the village did not have large houses. She lived with her husband and two kids and now had taken in the five of us, perhaps thinking that her brother would send her money from England that she could use to support her family as well as look after his five kids.

It didn't take too long before my aunt realized that my parents had no intention to send for the kids they had left behind in Jamaica. In fact, they had made no attempt to keep in touch or send any kind of financial support to us. It seemed that they had just abandoned us. My aunt was, of course, having none of it. Even though I was very young, I still remember her waking up day after day, doing nothing but fussing and quarreling and cussing at our parents for saddling her with five kids that she had no viable means of supporting. Her anger soon turned from being directed at our parents and to being taken out on us. Beatings and verbal abuse became the norm for us.

Needless to say, life was not very happy for us. We lived in constant fear of her anger since she could not get to our parents. The youngest sister was less than a year old and had to be looked after twenty-four hours each day. It was left up to the two oldest brothers—one nine and the other seven—to do so. Food was very limited, and there were days that we went with having nothing to eat. Hunger became a constant companion.

There was one particular incident that happened that made such an indelible imprint on me that it really stuck out in my mind. I was probably just about five years old at the time, but it is something that I still remember to this day as if it happened yesterday.

Our aunt had somehow gotten some food and was in the kitchen cooking soup. While she cooked, she was busy fussing and quarreling as was her norm. Her little house did not have a dining room, so we would sit on the rocks out in the yard to eat whenever we had food. This time, we were all sitting out in the yard anxiously waiting to get some soup. It had rained that afternoon, so the ground was wet and soggy. As we waited, we listened as she called our parents all manner of nasty names she could think of while making sure that we heard what she thought of us as well.

Finally, the soup was ready, and my two brothers, the oldest sister, and I sat outside in the yard waiting. I watched as my aunt picked up the pot from the fire in the outdoor kitchen, walked over to us sitting in the yard, and turned the pot of soup over into the mud while she angrily spit out these words at us, "Here, eat, you pigs."

5

As the soup sank into the mud, now totally inedible, the aroma of it wafted up to our hungry nostrils as we all sat there with sad faces, knowing that we would be going to bed hungry again another night.

Sometime after that, I do not know how long, word got to our parents in England that things were not going well with the kids and they needed to do something. What they did was to move us from that aunt to another aunt living in the village of Round Hill, where my parents were from. I do not know what promises were made to this particular aunt, but she agreed to take us all in to live with her in her little one-room shack. She and the girls slept on a bed on one side of the shack while the three boys slept on some rags strewn on the floor on the other side of the room.

We lived with her for about a year, and the thing I remembered was that she too was not receiving any financial support from our parents to help her with their five kids. On top of that, she was also an alcoholic.

Maybe it was because she was always drunk or because our parents still were not sending any support for their kids or maybe it was a combination of both, but she would beat us mercilessly. Whatever her reason was, all I knew at the time was that life for us was considerably more miserable than before.

Food was still very scarce except when mango season came around. The village had such a wide variety of mangoes that during the mango season, people had what they called "tun dun pat" (turn-down pot), which simply meant that no one did much of any cooking at all, as people relied mostly on mangoes to satisfy their hunger and would therefore turn down their pots since they were not going to be using them much for cooking. I don't remember ever going hungry during mango season. There were always ripe mangoes somewhere in the village that we could find to eat.

Because I was the smallest of my brothers, the oldest would climb the mango tree, pick the mangoes, eat off most of the flesh, and then throw down the seed to me with what was left on the seed. I had to quickly learn how to catch so that that precious mango seed did not fall to the ground and become inedible. It did not take me long to realize that if I was going to have my own mangoes, I needed to learn how to throw to pick my own since I was too small to climb the trees. And sure enough, it was not long before I could throw a rock accurately enough to be able to pick a single ripe mango from a bunch of green ones. I didn't need my brother's leftovers anymore.

Despite moving to live with a different aunt, things did not improve much. In fact, they might have gotten worse. Another of my father's sisters, seeing the terrible conditions we were living in and she herself being unable to offer much help, contacted the government welfare department to make them aware of our plight. The welfare department came to investigate, saw the situation, and took us away from our drunken aunt.

A Place of Horrors

My two sisters were sent to a home for girls, and the three boys were sent to a home for juvenile delinquent boys.

So here I was at seven years old, sharing a dormitory with boys who were much older than I was and many of whom were violent offenders.

Punishment for any offense at this juvenile facility was very harsh, especially so when you are just a seven-year-old boy. Many offenses were punishable by what was called "knee drill." The offending boy was required to fold his arms across his chest and then would alternate going down on his knees and getting up and going down again and again in the gravel in the road. This he would have to do for a minimum of half an hour or an hour depending on how serious the offense was.

During the day, all the boys had to work on the farm to plant and then harvest the crops. While I was there, there were boys who found the conditions too much for them and they would run away. When they were caught, they would be sent off to a regular prison rather than back to the juvenile facility. I hated the place. For me, the only difference was that we now had food to eat on a regular basis. But life for me was still miserable.

After about a year, my brothers and I were told that were we going to be reunited with our sisters and would be sent to an orphanage for both boys and girls. I was not disappointed to get away from that place and get to see my two little sisters again.

We moved to the orphanage when I was about eight years old. Living conditions there were a little better, but we still lived in dormitories with much bigger boys. It was while at this orphanage that I was repeatedly raped by much bigger boys. I was confused by all of this and unable to fight back or understand what was going on, and so I grew into a very angry young man. I knew nothing about what to do about that kind of abuse, and it continued for the full year I was there.

I do not know if a similar situation was happening with my two brothers because we never talked about it, and it was not something that I even talked about until I was an adult, married, and with children of my own.

A Home at Last

AFTER ABOUT A year of living at the orphanage, we were told that we were moving and going to live with foster parents. I had no idea what that meant, but on April 21, 1961, all five of us went to live with an elderly couple about one hundred miles away from the orphanage.

Our new foster parents were an older couple named Mr. and Mrs. Joseph. People affectionately called her Aunt Mar, but we all called her Mother. She was the one who ran the house. Her husband was sickly and mostly spent his day sitting on the veranda looking out.

Their house was like a palace to us. We had never been in a house that size before. It had four bedrooms, a living room, a dining room, and a huge veranda. There was an outdoor kitchen, and since it was in the country, there was an outdoor toilet. The house was situated on about twenty acres of land that was full of a variety of fruits for us to pick and eat. We were ecstatic!

The time from April to August of that year was perhaps some of the most wonderful times of my entire life up to then because all we did was run around the property and enjoy ourselves, playing games and enjoying as much fruit as we could eat. In addition, we also had regular meals every day so we were never hungry.

It was while living in our new foster home that we were taught some valuable life lessons as well. Our foster mother insisted that we take regular baths, brush our teeth, and do regular chores around the house. My primary responsibility was to help her in the kitchen, and that was how I learned to cook.

Each Saturday, it was the three boys' responsibility to go and get firewood that would be used for cooking during the week. We also had to make sure that we cut the grass in the yard using a machete and milk the one cow daily we had on the property. For us, life was good at last. We were all together, we had food enough to eat, and even though our foster parents were pretty strict, we were not being abused to the extent that had been the case in the past. As far as I was concerned, compared to my past living arrangements, life could not have been better.

That is not to say everything was perfect. Like I said before, we had many chores that we had to do. The one that I most hated was when once a month, our foster mother would wake up the boys to walk about four miles in the dark to meet a bus going to Montego Bay to send a package for her sister.

Now, running around playing during the day was one thing, but having to walk four miles in the dark was quite another. During the many times we made that journey in the three years I lived with my foster parents, I don't recall us having a single conversation as we walked in the dark to go meet the bus. We were so afraid of the dark that the only sound you heard from us was the sound of our bare feet walking along the gravel roads.

The bus would arrive at a particular place at about 6:30 a.m., so we had to make sure we walked fast enough to get there on time. By the time the bus came and we delivered the package, the sun would be coming up over the horizon, so we would walk back home in daylight with happy conversations among us. "Going to bus," as we called it, was my least favorite thing to do.

It's Not a Choice

AND THEN SEPTEMBER 1961 came! That was when our foster mother informed us that we would be going to school. School had never been a regular part of our lives, so having to go each day rather than being able to just run around and have fun was not something that I, for one, was looking forward to. But she insisted that was going to happen, and so she registered two of us in school in September of 1961.

Even though I was nearly ten years old, I could not read or write and so I was placed in first grade.

The schoolhouse itself consisted of two large open rooms, and each class was separated from the other by nothing but chalkboards. One of the rooms housed grades one through three and the other grades four through six. To this day, I am amazed how anyone could learn anything in that environment since the noise was constant and you were always aware of what was happening with the class right next to yours. But learn I did.

At the end of my first year, I was allowed to skip second grade and go on to third. At the end of third grade, I was allowed to skip fourth and go straight to fifth grade. The same thing was happening with my second brother, the one born before me. He started in third grade and then skipped to fifth grade. My oldest brother was not so fortunate. By the time we started school in 1961, he was already thirteen years old, and so our foster mother decided that he would be sent to learn the trade of carpentry. To this day, he has not learned to read or write properly, and he never did learn to do carpentry either.

The remarkable thing about learning, for my second brother and me, was that very few people in our immediate family had ever learned to read or write. My father had seventeen brothers and sisters and only two of them ever learned to read and write. My father never learned to read and write, and my mother, though she could read and write, had only gone through the sixth grade in primary school.

I don't recall, in the few years we spent with our parents, that they had any interest in sending us to school. We had to work with them on the little family farm they had before they packed up and went to England. Survival, it seems, was the primary goal for them, not school. And so, they didn't send us to school while they were with us, and while living in the juvenile facility and the orphanage, I had no interest whatsoever in going to school. That was why I was so disappointed on that September day in 1961 when our foster mother insisted that we were going to start going to school and it was not going to be up for discussion.

But now, here I was, the top student in my class two years in a row. At the beginning of my year in fifth grade, the principal of the school felt that I had the potential to sit and pass the nationwide exam that was necessary to go to high school. That meant that I would have to stay after school for extra tutoring to prepare for the exam. I did not want any part of that! After school was playtime for me, and all my friends would have gone home and I would still be stuck in a classroom with a teacher learning all I could by rote.

He Wasn't Asking

BACK IN THE early 1960s, there were no textbooks for students to study from. Instead, everything you learned was from what the teacher wrote on the chalkboard or said to you. After spending all day in a noisy classroom, I did not care about extra classes, much less have any desire to go to high school.

It wasn't long after these extra classes began that I started skipping them and going straight home after school dismissal. When I did go, it was obvious to the teacher that I didn't have much interest in what she was trying to teach me, and she told the principal that she did not wish to waste her time on me anymore. The principal called me and gave me what could only be described as a stern talking-to. He was quite adamant that I was going to start attending those classes regularly or else. And knowing the kind of person he was, I was not about to defy him. So to after-school classes, I went.

In the history of that particular primary school, only one student had ever been successful in passing that nationwide exam and gone on to high school. And the reason was simple: for the majority of people who sent their kids there, high school was a bridge too far. Their hope was that their kids would acquire some basic knowledge that could benefit them in their lives when they became adults. But as far as having their kids go on to high school, that was at best a wild dream since it was not something they could afford.

Besides, the nearest high school was at least three to four hours away, which meant the child would have to get up and drive to and from school for eight hours each day—something that was not viable since few, if any, of these parents owned vehicles. The alternative would be to board the child with someone near the school. But again, this too was still not a viable alternative since that would take money and the vast majority of these people were poor, some very, very poor.

Even if a student was able to get a scholarship where the government paid for their tuition, every other cost would have to be borne by the parents, and again, this was money that they just did not have. It was no wonder that not many students had ever even attempted to take that exam to try to get into high school.

However, my principal insisted that I was smart enough to take and pass that exam. How I was going to pay the cost associated with going to high school, I had no idea. And so out of fear of him and not wanting the teacher to continue being angry with me for wasting her time, I started going to the after-school classes every day.

I sat the exam on January 28, 1964. I had just turned twelve years old. To this day, I have no memory of a single question that was on the exam paper or a single answer I gave. All I know is that I went and did the exam, forgot about it, and was just very happy that I no longer had to go to any more after-school classes. And when I say I forgot about it, I really did. I had no idea when the results were to be published or announced nor did I care. It was back to living my regular life for me.

An Unlikely Hero

IT MIGHT HAVE been about April of 1964 when I suddenly began to have some throbbing pain on one side of my face. I ignored it at first, but after about two months, it had gotten so bad that my foster mother insisted that I go and have it checked. The nearest doctor was at the hospital which was about fifty miles away, and to get there, I would have to walk about four miles to get a bus to take me there. And so one morning, my foster mother gave me the fare for the bus, and I set out to get to the place where I would take the bus.

I got there on time to get the bus and got to the hospital. I was twelve years old and had never been in a hospital before, so while I don't recall how, I somehow ended up seeing a nurse who, after I told her what the problem was, gave me a pill to take and then sent me back home. It did nothing for the pain, and so I went and waited outside the hospital gate for when the bus would be going back my way again, got on, and then got off at the place where I would begin the four-mile walk to my home.

My foster mother had told me to stop at the store near where I got off the bus and buy her a newspaper on my way back home. She would, from time to time, send us to buy the newspaper at that store. After she read the newspaper, she would then allow us kids to look through it, after which it was stored under her bed to be used as toilet paper in the outdoor toilet.

Back then, when we picked up the newspaper, we were warned not to read out everything in the newspaper before we brought it home. I, for one, was under the impression that if I read something in the newspaper before my foster mother read it, it would disappear, and she would not have it to read. This was not true, of course, but I guess the idea was to make sure we kids kept the newspaper neatly folded and got it back in one piece.

Anyway, after I picked up the newspaper, I began browsing through it and noticed that there were pages with a long list of names printed in it. It was then I realized that these were the names of all the students throughout the island who had taken the national exam and passed it.

When I was chosen to sit for the exam, I was asked to name the high school I wanted to attend. I had named the most popular and well-known high school in the capital city. I did not hold out much hope that I would ever get to go there, so I began looking at names for those who had won a scholarship to this particular high school, and when I didn't see my name, I folded up the newspaper and started my trek home.

As I slowly made my way home, still with that throbbing pain in my face, I became aware that people were shouting my name and saying "Congratulations." I was puzzled. I thought they were making fun of me or something.

"Congratulations for what?" I asked.

"Haven't you heard?" someone shouted.

"Heard what?" was my response.

"You got a scholarship to Manning's High School!" was the response.

What! I was perplexed.

I quickly opened the newspaper again and looked for Manning's High School. I had never heard of that school before, and after I found the school's name, I began searching for my name. And there it was written in black on white, my first, middle, and my last name in the national newspaper.

It had been years since anyone had successfully passed that exam from that primary school, and suddenly, I was the most well-known person in the entire area. People came from all over to congratulate my foster mother on my success. Even my teachers and the principal looked at me and treated me differently. I had somehow become an unwitting hero for the school and the people in the little village where we lived. I had achieved what many had only dreamed about. I had won a scholarship. I was going to high school, and somehow that made me special.

How I had managed to go from first grade to high school in just three years is still a mystery to me. I have no idea how I was able to learn things well enough without textbooks to be able to pass a national exam. At the time, in 1964 Jamaica, only about twenty-three hundred students nationwide were chosen to get scholarships to go to high school each year. Now I was one of the few blessed to be chosen.

It was as if everything changed for me from that moment on. For one thing, the pain in my face disappeared completely, and I walked the rest of the way home free from pain but with a smile permanently etched on my face and the constant shouts of congratulations ringing in my ears.

Later on in my life, I would come to realize that my ability to learn could only have been a gift from the Lord. Only he could have allowed what happened to me to happen, and to this day and forever, I will be eternally grateful!

Two Most Remarkable People

BEING A WARD of the court meant that it was not my foster parents but the government's responsibility to provide me with what I needed to attend school, including finding a place for me to board. The idea was for me to board with a family in the town where the school was located and then return to my foster home during breaks from school.

And that was how after taking me for the weekend to buy the clothing and other things I would need, the welfare officer and I headed to orientation at the high school campus that September Saturday morning in 1964.

We were late, the orientation was over, and so we set out to find the place where I would be boarding.

I have no idea why we were late. I still have no idea why I was adamant that I did not want to live in that particular house. I still have no idea why the welfare officer agreed with me, and I still am clueless as to why he drove back up to the school rather than somewhere else. And I never did ask why the Meads, after meeting me for the very first time, chose to take me into their home to live with them. I can only put it all down to what a verse in Romans 8:28 says, "All things work together for good."

While I was living in foster care, the government would always send a monthly check to help take care of us. After I went to live with the Meads, they received no such checks. In fact, in the six years I lived with the Meads, I can recall only once that anyone from the government came to check on me. It was as if they knew that I had found a true family, and I didn't need the help of the government anymore.

No two people have had a greater impact on my life than Mr. and Mrs. Mead. Until I came to live with them that September day in 1964, I had never met two more generous and caring people. And since then, there have been very few people indeed that I would put in the same category of importance to me as these two.

My recollection of the story of my life with the Meads is that of a time of love, caring, and belonging.

The Meads had come from England to Jamaica at the invitation of some Christian friends who thought they could help in the development of the country through their gift as teachers.

Mr. Mead was a true renaissance man in every sense of the word. He was educated, well-read, knew, and could quote from memory long portions of Shakespeare's plays. In addition, he sang, could play the piano, and taught chemistry, biology, physics, and mathematics at the high school level. He developed the school's cadet unit (ROTC) that was voted the best cadet unit in the country two years in a row while I was in high school.

In addition, he also started a chapter of the Interschool Christian Fellowship (ISCF) on campus that met every Sunday afternoon. He was a deacon and Sunday school teacher in his church and would often fill in as the speaker when the pastor was unavailable.

He was chosen to be the assistant principal and later the principal of the high school.

He was perhaps the most selfless person I had ever met. Here was a man who would go and pick up students who wanted to attend ISCF meetings each Sunday afternoon and then made sure they got back home safely. During school exam times, if a student lived too far away and would probably arrive too late by bus, Mr. Mead would voluntarily go and pick up that student to make sure they would be on time for their exam.

In my eyes, he was truly the most remarkable man I had ever met. He represented nothing like I had seen before in my young life. I had mostly seen men who drank, cussed a lot, and abused their wives and children. But here was a man who was kind and loving toward his wife and around whom his kids were comfortable and at ease. I truly loved the man. To me, he was an exceptional human being.

Now, while Mrs. Mead might not have been as gifted as her husband in so many different areas, here too was a woman who was truly remarkable. She had to care for eight kids, and one of them was a virtual stranger to her. When I came to live with them, I was the oldest at twelve and yet I was never made to feel out of place or that I didn't belong. She ran the house, and everything seemed to always go so smoothly and well. I don't recall any crisis that was not handled and solved for all eight kids. She was a teacher like her husband and taught art and English. She too played the piano and was very good with people.

I don't think I have ever met anyone who did not like and appreciate the Meads.

Their children were true Jamaicans too. They had all adapted well to the culture and could speak the dialect as well as any Jamaican. They fit right in despite the fact that they were English.

The contribution of Mr. and Mrs. Mead to the development of thousands of Jamaican children is immeasurable.

Looking back now, I know that it probably was not as easy for the Meads to receive me into their family as it might have appeared to me. I was a country bumpkin at best, hardly able to speak proper English, and was certainly not well schooled in all the aspects of good manners and proper etiquette. I am sure that I must have behaved in ways that caused them some discomfort at times. And yet they never gave up on me. They persisted and took what was a twelve-year-old who had endured much trauma and helped to shape him in such a way that he was able live a productive life and thus was able to help to shape the lives of many of those with whom he would come in contact during the course of his life.

Their influence on all of us is clearly evident by the fact that of the eight of us kids, six became teachers, one became a minister, and the other a nurse. All of us in the business of serving and helping others just like they did.

Despite their loving care of me, there was one thing that happened in the Meads' household that I was never able to feel a part of. Most mornings and more so on the weekends, the Mead kids would all wake up and run into their parents' bedroom and pile into the bed with them. I would often walk up to the bedroom door and watch them as they chatted away, lying in their parent's arms, but I never felt that I could or should do that. It was as if at those times, I recognized that I was different and had come from a different background. I had never seen kids being able to just run into their parents' room and jump on their bed while laughing with utter delight before. That was new to me.

But what I did take from seeing that was that when I had my kids, I made sure that they knew they were free to run into my bedroom and pile into the bed with me and chat and laugh and watch television with their dad.

A Different World

HIGH SCHOOL WAS indeed a truly different world for me. When I started high school, my ability to speak or write the English language well was very limited. I was accustomed to speaking only the Jamaican dialect (patois) on a regular basis, so coming to high school where I was required to speak and write properly was a new experience. And here was another instance where living with the Meads undoubtedly helped me a lot. They had a library in the house with a lot of books. Each night before we went to bed, Mrs. Mead would read to us, and the children, even though they spoke the Jamaican dialect, always spoke proper English with their parents at home.

It was not only English that was a challenge. So too were certain subjects with which I was not acquainted, none more so than Spanish and French. These were truly foreign languages to me, but for the very first time, I actually had textbooks to use to learn from.

I had homework. I never knew there was such a thing until I got to high school. In primary school, the emphasis had always being on the three Rs: Reading, 'Riting, and 'Rithmetic, with some history and Bible knowledge thrown in. But in high school, I was confronted with some serious subjects that I had never studied or read about before. In addition to French and Spanish, I also studied chemistry, biology, and physics.

I truly believe I was only able to navigate my way through high school successfully because of the family I had become a part of. I could always receive help with any subject matter I had. Mr. Mead was a walking encyclopedia, as far as I was concerned, and along with his wife, there was no subject matter that they couldn't provide help with when we needed it. In addition, there were always other teachers coming and going through the house all the time. So they were also available to help.

Living with teachers also meant that there was always going to be scrutiny of how we were doing, and each semester, a school report was sent home indicating how well we were doing in our classes.

All through high school, I was usually a member of classes that averaged about thirty-two students, and at the end of each school year, each student was ranked according to their academic performance in the class for the year. The lowest I remember being ranked was sixteenth out of thirty-two. All the other times, I was always ranked in the top ten of my class.

I do not know if it was because the Meads were so huge in my eyes, but I have no recollection of the names of any of my other teachers during my years in high school except for one. His family and everyone else called him Stalin, but his real name was Alvin Surgeon. He was my history teacher in first form, my first year of high school.

I remember that for my first midterm exam, I had scored only a 32 percent on his history test. But for the finals, I scored a 97 percent. When I got my test paper back, Mr. Surgeon had crossed out the 97 and replaced it with a 92. When I inquired as to why, his response was "Boy, nobody gets a 97 on my test."

The result of that test was what motivated me to develop a passion for reading and a love of history. It was Mr. Surgeon who motivated me to love history so much that I would make it my major in teachers' college and then taught the subject in middle and high school for many years. There were other subjects that I liked too, like English literature and geography, but my love of history began in my first year in high school with my first-form teacher, Mr. Alvin Surgeon.

I would often hear people lament how much they hated history while in school. I could never understand that. In fact, I have always felt that a person's education was not complete unless they had studied history.

So Much to Do

It was in high school that I also developed a great love of sports and other activities. When I began school in 1964, cricket was the only sport I had ever played. I was pretty good at it too. I was the only first year student up to that time to make the school's first eleven cricket team (the equivalent of making the varsity team). I was only thirteen, stood only four feet nine inches tall, and was chosen by the coach to be the opening batsman for the team, much to the chagrin of all the other members who were all seniors and did not appreciate having a first-former on the team.

But cricket was not my only love. If an activity was happening on campus, I wanted to participate in it. Apart from cricket, I would go on to represent the school in football (soccer), track and field, table tennis, and drama. I was second in command of the cadet unit when it was voted the most outstanding unit in the country two years in a row and was among those chosen to go on a cadet exchange to Canada in 1968.

Being chosen for that trip to Canada was very special for me. Each year, cadets from across the island would gather at Up Park Camp, the home of the Jamaica Defense Force (JDF), to be put through a series of activities. At the end of which, cadets were chosen to represent the island in Canada, the Bahamas, Trinidad and Tobago, and Barbados. Getting selected to go to Canada was considered to be the most prestigious destination. I was shocked when I was chosen since the sergeant in charge had made it a point to belittle me as much as possible for the entire week we were there. He once told me in front of all the other cadets that I would have to do twice as well just to be sent back home, much less to be chosen to go overseas. Well, I showed him.

I was table tennis captain, cricket captain, tennis singles champion, house captain, and school prefect. I was also very active with the Interschool Christian Fellowship (ISCF) and performed with the drama club.

Sports and other extracurricular activities kept me occupied. Part of the reason was that I was not a person with many friends. I often had a chip on my shoulder because I was very self-conscious of the fact that I had not grown up with my parents, and this was a source of much ridicule from some people. Being active and busy gave me focus.

Perhaps my most memorable accomplishment in sports was at the national boys' athletics championship held at the National Stadium in 1968. I had been chosen to represent my school in the discus.

Before the national championships, there were regional championships, and I easily won the discus competition for class 2 boys at regional. At the national championship, these were the best from around the island. Each boy was initially given six throws, and from that, they would chose the top six who would be given an extra three throws to determine the winner. I was down to my very last throw in the initial six when I reeled off the longest throw I had ever thrown a discus and went from dead last to second, and that was my final position. Second in the discus for class 2 boys in the national athletics championships for high school boys in the entire country was quite an achievement for me. Back then, they didn't give out medals. You would get a certain number of points for your position which would then be added to your school's total points to determine the ultimate winner of the championship.

While the girls at Manning's High School were able to win the national championship several times, the boys never did.

Pass or Bust

My FIFTH YEAR in high school was a really busy one for me. Each student was required to sit for the Cambridge University O Level exam, and how successful you were in passing individual subjects in the exam would indicate how successful your time in high school had been. It was also a good indicator of how successful you were probably going to be in your future endeavors.

A student having passes in at least five subjects was considered successful. But if you wanted to go on to a sixth and seventh year in high school to prepare you for entrance to university, you had to do substantially better than just passing five subjects. You had to have a minimum of five subjects, but they would all have to be passes with distinctions, not just ordinary passes. It meant intensive studies to make sure that you would do your absolute best when the exam came around.

Year five then was an important transitionary year for all students. If you failed to pass any subject at all and you were eighteen years old or older, you had to leave school and somehow hope that you could find a job where the employer did not require any passes in the exam. For a good job, that was going to be a highly unlikely scenario. You would be considered a failure, leaving high school with nothing to show for it. If you were under eighteen and if the principal would allow it, you could repeat your fifth year and try to be more successful in the exam the next time.

If you hoped to go on to university, going on for the next two years in high school was a must. Only the very smartest got to go on.

It was during my fifth year that I was the busiest. I had been appointed cricket captain, and that meant supervising all practices. I was table tennis captain, second in command of the cadet unit, a school prefect, and represented the school in soccer and athletics as well.

I graduated high school in June of 1969. I was seventeen years old and had my five passes in the Cambridge University O level exam but had only two distinctions. The principal told me he would allow me to repeat my fifth year if I wanted, but I had other pressing things to be concerned with then and so I refused the offer.

Alone Again, Naturally

THE YEAR 1969 began to see some major changes in life for me.

Mr. Mead had been appointed the principal of the school in the middle of some major cultural upheaval that was occurring in Jamaica at the time. Many people, particular the young, were becoming more and more culturally aware. The "black is beautiful" and "black power" craze that was sweeping across American had arrived with full force in Jamaica. And with that came some hostility to those who were not black. Mr. Mead, being white, was not immune to this hostility.

Despite the fact that he had given ten years of his life faithfully serving in the school and the community, there were still those who resented him simply because of the color of his skin. So out of concern for the well-being of his family, he resigned from his position as principal and returned to England with the family.

Although I had been considered a part of the family for six years, going with them to England was not an option for me since by this time, I was eighteen years old and considered an adult.

The six years I lived with the Meads were the longest I had ever lived with anyone, including my parents. So when they left, I was now really on my own with no family around to support or help me. Despite that, I did have in mind what I wanted to do going forward.

I had just spent nine straight years in school and felt that I needed a break, so I quickly found a job in a sugar factory where I worked for a year. After that, I worked for another year as an accounting clerk for Singer Sewing Machine Company.

But what kept constantly ringing in my ears was what Mrs. Mead had drilled in me before she left. "Go to college! You must go on to college!" Over and over again, she would remind me that if I wanted to achieve anything in life, a college education was paramount.

Having graduated from high school with only two distinctions, I knew that university was out of the question for me at that point. I just wasn't academically qualified to be accepted at the only university on the island, the University of the West Indies. The only college I was qualified for was teachers' college, and so one year after the Meads left me on my own in Jamaica, I started college to become a teacher at Church Teachers College in Mandeville.

That Girl

I HAD TWO girlfriends in high school. One was named Mimby and the other one everyone referred to her as Darling. Apparently, the name stemmed from the fact that her grandparents thought she was such a darling when she was a baby, and the name just stayed with her as she grew up. She was a beautiful girl, and maybe that was the reason I was attracted to her. Mimby was also a very pretty girl and was very much smarter than Darling.

There was not much of a social life to be had in the town of Sav-la-Mar where I lived, and many of the students who attended the high school either drove in or biked in from miles away. That was the case with Mimby and Darling. They both lived at least ten miles or more away from school, so right after school ended, they would set out on their bike or get on the bus to go back home.

Darling was my first crush, and the extent of our relationship was to talk at school and for me to walk her to the bus to go home. Since Mimby rode a bike, I would often walk with her for some distance before I would have to turn around and head back home. There were no places of interest to go on a date, and most of my time after school was taken up with extracurricular activities. I guess having a girlfriend was like a rite of passage for guys in my school since we knew nothing about dating.

After being friends for about a year, Darling decided to move on with her life. That was fine with me, and soon after that, I developed a crush on Mimby. Now to be honest, these were at best schoolboy crushes. They were never anything serious, and so by the time I graduated high school, these girls were no longer a part of my conscious thoughts.

And then one day, for no apparent reason, I borrowed one of the Mead boys' bike and just set off riding down into the town and ended up at a friend's house. We were good friends, and I knew his mother and knew that he had a brother and two sisters. I rode into his yard and found out that he was not there, but his oldest sister was. Like me, she attended the same high school and went to the same church, but that was the extent of any interaction between us.

I got off my bike and sat down on her veranda, and we just began talking and that was when I really began to take any serious notice of her. I realized that she really was a beautiful girl. Short but beautiful, and she really had my attention. I liked her immediately, and from that day, we became inseparable. One was rarely ever seen without the other. She became that girl for me!

Nicky was the first girl to really capture my total attention. She was good to look at, had similar moral values to mine, was great to talk to, and she lived just a short distance from my home. She still had one year to go to complete high school, so each day after school, we would meet and talk, and I would help with her homework and studying for her exams.

An Ignorant Old Fart

I HAD NEVER encountered any form of prejudice until I went to live with the Meads. Since the Meads were white, I noticed that there were people who were making a conscious effort to cultivate their friendship. There was one well-to-do white family in the town of Sav-la-Mar who apparently very much wanted the Meads to be counted among their circle of friends. Being teachers and not making a lot of money, the Meads didn't have much in common with this particular family except for their white skin. I remembered that soon after I went to live with the Meads, they received an invitation to dinner with this particular family with the stipulation that I was not to come with the rest of the family. Apparently, they wanted only white people seated around their family table eating. Mrs. Mead's response was firm and unequivocal: either we all went or none of us would go. We didn't go.

There were several people who lived in the town of Sav-la-Mar who Jamaicans would describe as being "high colored," which simply meant that they were so fair-skinned that some of them could easily pass as white. Many of them were of the notion that that made them superior to their fellow black Jamaican. In fact, the idea that darker skin meant you were the lesser had been ingrained in people from the time of slavery. And even some one hundred years after the end of slavery in Jamaica, there were still people who felt that if a person married someone who was fair-skinned, they had married up, so to speak.

There were people in Sav-la-Mar who would not give someone like me the time of day. They would probably answer if I said "Good morning," but that would be the extent of any personal interaction with these people.

I remember one such family and their daughter, and yet years later, when I returned to Jamaican with a doctoral degree and being appointed the headmaster of one of the more prestigious high schools on the island, it was as if we were old friends from back in the day. It was all right now to try to foster a friendship with me because I was educated and had influence and position, but I had no such desire.

Sav-la-Mar had a few such persons, and it just so happened that Nicky's father was one. Ethnically, he was a mix of white and Indian. He had been married to a white woman before he married Nicky's mother and the man was totally illiterate. But this did not stop him from thinking that his ethnicity made him superior to the blacks around him. Not surprisingly, he had a fit when he found out that I was dating his daughter. He made his displeasure known by carrying around an ice pick with which he would threaten me every time I would walk Nicky home. When he saw me coming, he would make sure to walk off his veranda to his gate with ice pick in hand to make sure I didn't come through the gate.

In the years I had lived with the Meads, I had become pretty well-known in Sav-la-Mar as an athlete as well as being active in my church. People knew me to be a principled young man. Among them was the pastor of my church. So many people tried to reason with him to point out that his reaction to me was unfair and without merit. Even his white children from his first wife went and spoke to him on my behalf. But for three years, it made no difference to him.

Despite her father's objection, Nicky and I grew closer and closer. But I still was not allowed to visit her at home. I don't recall being angry or mad with her father during this time. I think it was more that I pitied him for his ignorance more than anything. And besides, how he felt did not affect the way I felt about his daughter. I was in love.

I still do not know the specific reason, but one day, I got a message that he wanted me to come and see him and so I went. We spoke for quite some time, and it was then I told him that I intended to marry his daughter. His demeanor changed at that point to being a lot friendlier toward me. After we talked, I began to realize that part of his original objection was that he thought I was just like many of the other men he knew who got young girls pregnant and then move on. He did not want that for his daughter.

I assured him that I was not like that, and apparently, many of the people, who had spoken to him before on my behalf, had attested to my character as a principled young man. I took the opportunity then and there to ask his permission to marry his daughter. He agreed and even suggested that we live in his house until we got properly settled since at that time, both Nicky and I still had to complete our final year in college.

And so, one very soggy Saturday afternoon in August 1972, Nicky's father, who for more than three years was adamant that I not even walk through his gate, walked his daughter down the aisle and gave her hand to me in marriage.

Not What I Expected

PRIOR TO GETTING married, in late August 1971, I arrived on campus at Church Teachers' College to begin my training to become a teacher. No one in my family background had ever gone to college, much less studied to be a teacher. And so I knew that my desire to become a teacher could only have come from being with the Meads. I had seen the tremendous impact they had on their students. I had no idea if I had any ability to be a teacher. All I knew was that I wanted to be like Mr. Mead, a man I held in the highest estimation possible.

I had persuaded Nicky to enroll in teachers' college as well, but she chose to go to a college that was for women only, mine was a co-ed college.

I had arrived on campus with all the new students for a one-week orientation before classes began. Along with meeting the instructors, the student body president was also on campus that week to help us understand all the ins and outs of college life. The week went by pretty quietly and uneventfully. I supposed that all of us were pretty nervous being in a new environment. But all the people we encountered that week were very pleasant and very helpful.

All that changed the night the seniors arrived on campus.

Back in 1971, teacher training included two years of college and one year of internship, where you actually went out and taught in a classroom for one year before you would receive your college diploma indicating that you were now a certified teacher.

So for your first year, you were regarded as a freshman or a "grub" as we were called by the seniors, and for your second year, you became a senior. Seniors ruled the campus. Hazing—or ragging as it was called—was the norm, and most freshmen suffered much abuse at the hands of these seniors, especially in the first month on campus.

The abuse started the very first night they arrived on campus. Immediately, we were being called nasty names that were designed to make it clear that we were only grubs (freshmen) and subjected to the whims of the seniors.

I was flabbergasted at the behavior of these seniors. What was even more surprising to me was that a lot of the abuse was being led by the females. I had never seen women behave like that before, and it was hard for me to believe that these were the people who being so raucous and disgusting in their words and behavior were going to be teachers. I had expected to encounter well-mannered and courteous people. To me, they were more like hooligans than anything else. I was dumbfounded!

The night they arrived on campus, it was the custom that the freshmen would arrange for and serve refreshments to the seniors during the intermission of a concert that the freshmen were required to put on for them as well.

I was chosen to be the master of ceremony for the first part of the concert, and I didn't have a chance. Before I could open my mouth to introduce any of the participants, they were on their feet shouting, hooting, booing, and making all sorts of nasty comments. This continued all through the first part of the concert, and I was not only frustrated, but by then, I had become angry, very, very angry.

At the beginning of the intermission, I announced that there were refreshments specially prepared for the seniors in the dining room. From the abuse that they rained down on me that night, you would have thought I had just cussed out their mama.

For the concert, all the seniors sat in the back of the room and all the freshmen had to sit up front. That was the way things were done, but I didn't know that. And so, at the intermission, I ventured to the back of the room to speak to the student body president whom we had met during the week and whom I thought was one of the most pleasant people I had ever met. I wanted to express my disgust to him about the behavior of these seniors. I didn't get a chance to get near him. When they saw that a freshman had invaded their space the abuse became louder and more vulgar.

Having spent time in an orphanage, I had seen bullying. I had been the target of bullies, and I hated it. To this day, I don't think there is anything I despise more than a bully. I was never a violent person, but at that stage of my life, anger still came easily to me and so when they started in on me, instead of being intimidated, I looked around for one of the guys who was being the loudest and the more obnoxious. I went right up to him, pointed my finger in his face, and said, "If you mess with me one more time, I will 'carn' your ass right here!"

You could have heard a pin drop. Everyone was shocked that a freshman had the audacity to dare speak to a senior like that. But I didn't care. I had had it with their abuse and vulgarity and just wasn't going to have any more of it. I walked out and went back to the front of the room with their shouted abuses ringing in my ears.

After that night, not a single senior tried to haze me or abuse me in any way for my entire freshman year. I would learn later that there were many of them that had wanted to do me harm, but because I shared a room with the most intimidating senior on the campus, Mitchy, none of them dared come to my room to try anything. And so, while other freshmen were suffering much abuse at the hands of seniors, including things like being woken up at two and three in the morning and made to stand outside in the cold with nothing on but their underwear, I slept through the nights with no interruptions.

Young and Foolish

GROWING UP, I always had a problem with acceptance. The fact that my parents left me and that my aunts did not particularly like having me and my brothers and sisters around really impacted the way I felt about myself and the way I expected others to accept me. On top of that, I was always teased mercilessly about the color of my eyes. Growing up black with light eyes, people called me "puss eye" because of the colors of my eyes. I hated the colors of my eyes because of that. In fact, it wasn't until I was nearly thirty years old that I was made aware that there were people who found my eyes attractive.

After I moved from Jamaica to New York, I went to the DMV to get my license. As this elderly white lady was taking down my information, she asked me for my eye color. I didn't know what to tell her, and I certainly wasn't going to say "puss eyes." Seeing my hesitation, she looked up, looked at my eyes, and shouted at one of her coworkers, "Come and look at this, a black man with hazel eyes."

So that was the color eyes I have, not puss eyes, I remember thinking. She then went on to tell me that I had beautiful eyes. This was the first time anyone had complimented me on my eye color.

So for nearly thirty eyes I had lived with the dread of having unusually colored eyes that I was not proud of, and now I was finding out that people found them attractive because they were not puss eyes but hazel. Well, what do you know?

Moving from one government facility to an orphanage to a foster home did not free me from my sense of lack of acceptance.

Even after I went to live with the Meads and I could see how much they cared for me, I was always suspicious as to whether I, a little black boy, could ever be fully accepted into a white family where they already had seven children of their own.

I finally began to feel a sense of acceptance after I met Nicky and we became inseparable. When we got married, I was only twenty years old and she was just nineteen. Looking back, I realize now that I knew absolutely nothing about marriage or being a husband or a father at age twenty. I just thought, *Here was someone who had accepted me*, and I was very happy for that. It wasn't long after the wedding that things began to change.

We were honeymooning in Negril, and the Sunday morning after the wedding, we had gone walking on the beach when I saw her brother approaching. Being newlyweds, I had my arms around her and was attempting to kiss her when she pushed me away. *Wow*, I thought. *What is this? That's new! She had never done that before.*

From that day forward, I never felt like things were the same with us as they were before we got married. On top of that, we had moved into her father's house, which we now share with him and her sister and brother. I was smart enough to quickly move out of that house into one of our own, but that sense of alienation never really left me.

It was as if I had become an afterthought to her. It appeared to me that her family's concerns and welfare were far more important to her than mine. This became so apparent to me one day after we had moved to Kingston to live. I had come home from work and was very hungry. I was glad to see that she had dinner ready. As I sat down and began to eat, she suddenly came and took up the plate of food from in front of me. Thinking that maybe she was going to put more food on my plate, I followed her into the kitchen. And there she was, taking a substantial amount of the food from my plate and putting it on another. When I inquired what she was doing, her response was that her brother was coming to visit, and she needed to have something for him to eat. Shocked would not be a strong enough word to describe my reaction.

I was young and foolish, I suppose, and I did not want to accept that I might have made a mistake. I did not want to accept failure, and so I stayed in a marriage that was not really good for me for nearly twenty-six years.

A Familiar Face

WHEN I STARTED primary school in 1961, I knew absolutely no one at the school. During the three years I attended, there were some students that I got to know pretty well. One such person was a pleasant boy named Headley from a little district (village) called Forrest Mountain. It was called that because it was up in the mountains, and every morning, a number of students could be seen coming down from up in the mountain to attend school. Usually, they would all arrive together.

Forrest Mountain was really like a little village where everyone knew everyone. People who lived there were typical of the people living in the surrounding areas. They didn't have much and would try to eke out a living for their family the best they knew how by growing some sort of crop. School was not a high priority for many of these people, and so it would not be unusual for students to miss days of school if their parents needed them to work on their family plot of land that they used for farming.

It was in primary school that I first met Headley. I remember him as a scrawny kid who did not say much. I don't remember having much interaction with Headley while in school. And so when I left to go to high school, I did not think that I would ever see him again. And I did not again until that August day in 1971 when I started attending teachers' college. The remarkable thing was that even though we hadn't seen each other for more than seven years, when we met again that day on campus, it was as if we were two old friends

42

who had only been away for just a few days. Headley and I became fast friends in a way that makes our friendship a pretty unusual one. He is very much a beloved brother to me. He is, without doubt, one of the most remarkable people I have ever known.

When I went off to high school, Headley had finished primary school but was not able to get into high school. But what he did was that he studied for the same exam high school students had to take at the end of their fifth year, and he had done well enough to qualify to get into teachers' college.

There were several very brilliant students at the college Headley and I was attending. There were students there who had passed up to ten individual subjects in the Cambridge University O level exam, a very difficult feat. And because the student body consisted of only one hundred and ten students, the college could afford to pick and choose from only the very best qualified to attend.

While Headley might not have had the best academic qualifications compared to others, I remember the day of graduation that the person who received the award for outstanding academic achievement was none other than Headley. He had outperformed the entire best student body on campus. That was the kind of person he is. On campus, he demonstrated all the attributes of hard work, diligence, exemplary behavior, and he was totally committed to his faith.

At the end of our first year in college, it was Headley whom we all voted for to be the new president of the student body. This scrawny kid, from a little village up in the mountain with no electricity or running water, had come to college and, with humility and tremendous work ethics, had outperformed us all.

Headley has always been such an example to me in faith and godliness. I have never seen him angry or rude to anyone. In all the years I have known him, I don't recall ever exchanging a harsh word with him. He is always calm and even keeled. He is the only person of whom I can truthfully say, "Here is a man in whom there is no guile."

To this day, Headley is still my best friend, and even though we don't get to see each other very often, when we do, it is like no time has passed since the last time we met. He is a brother that I truly love!

Apologize or Else

COLLEGE WAS NOT too difficult for me academically, but it did have its challenges. I was a nineteen-year-old from the country and coming into an environment that was totally different from what I was used to. I had lived a more or less sheltered life before then, and now here I was, being exposed to worldliness in a way I did not know.

My desire to live as a Christian young man on campus was a major challenge. I did not know before I went to college that there were young women who would actually proposition men. I was shocked at how openly sexual some of these college students were. They made no effort to hide their intentions and would laugh at you if you thought or wanted to behave differently. At best, you were considered a prude or, at worst, just stupid. Perhaps I was both a prude and stupid because at the end my first year in college, I decided to get married. As a young Christian, I felt that I didn't want to leave myself open to all the obvious temptations that were all around me.

And so it was that I arrived on campus to begin my second year of college with a new bride. Nicky had agreed to transfer from her college to mine so that we would be together. There were only a handful of married students, mostly women, since apart from myself, there was no other married man on campus. There were no facilities to accommodate a married couple, so we had to rent an apartment off campus to live.

Living off campus meant that I didn't get to be as involved with as many activities as before. Right after classes ended for the day, we would head home to our apartment.

That was the routine we would follow each day except when cricket season came around. Since I was one of the main members of the team, I would have to be there for practice and to play matches.

Nicky would stay on campus while I played and would often spend time in the Home Economics Department with the instructor since that was her major.

One day, as we made our way home, she mentioned that the instructor had been particularly rude to her and that got me very upset. I returned to the campus, found the instructor, and told her in no uncertain terms that I did not appreciate her treatment of my wife.

Again, in today's environment, that might not sound like a big deal, but this was Jamaica 1972. Teachers were still regarded with great respect. You didn't tell off or speak rudely to a teacher, even if you were an adult. I thought that all I had done was stand up for my wife.

The following morning, I was called to the college principal's office and asked to explain myself. I don't recall all that was said, but I remember being told that unless I made a public apology to the instructor in front of the entire student body, I was going to be asked to leave the college. I was going to be expelled.

I reluctantly agreed and so the following morning, I, a senior, had to stand up in front of my fellow seniors (as well as the freshmen) and apologize. I still remember the looks of shock and sadness on the faces of the students as I read my apology.

To say I felt humiliated would be an understatement, but that is precisely what I think the principal wanted to achieve. He felt that since I had humiliated a member of his staff by telling her off for being rude to my wife, then he was going to return the favor by humiliating me before the entire student body, including the freshmen.

After my apology, the instructor who had the run-in with my wife tried to make amends by trying to be more friendly to her, but at that particular time, I was not prepared to forgive her for her rudeness, especially in light of her having me humiliated by being made to apologize to her in front of everybody.

After I graduated, it would take another twenty-seven years before I would be invited back to that college campus to speak to the student body, and by that time, I was myself a high school principal.

You Reap What You Sow

APART FROM HEADLEY, I have made some great friends in college who have remained my friends to this day, more than fifty years later. Two such people were Donville and Ambie.

These two guys were probably among the most pleasant and smartest of the students on campus. Donville was much more outgoing and made friends easily; Ambie, on the other hand, was more on the quiet side. You probably would never hear him raise his voice in anger or lash out at anyone. In fact, he was such a gentle person that we nicknamed him Lamb, as in "gentle as a lamb."

Ambie had told us about some of his experience with bullying while in high school, particularly about one person who had bullied him relentlessly. So imagine our wonder of wonders, when at the beginning of our senior year, among the new grubs coming on campus was Ambie's tormentor. In high school, he was Ambie's senior, but now he was going to be Ambie's grub. I do not know what he must have thought that first day he walked on campus and saw that Ambie was going to be his senior, and now he was going to be at the mercy of the one whom he had bullied so badly in high school.

Still, Ambie was way too kind and forgiving to see it as an opportunity to exact vengeance on this guy. But that was not how his batch mates felt. This bully had to pay—and pay he did: for the first month on campus, he was subjected to all sorts of abuse and humiliation. It was as if there was added relish in doing uncomfortable things to him because they knew that he had in the past chosen to bully the Lamb.

Even though he was a pretty big guy, there was absolutely nothing he could do about it. He was now reaping what he had sown.

Because I did not live on campus, I did not participate in any ragging of the new grubs. I remembered how I hated seeing what the seniors did to my batch mates, and I did not feel that ragging was something I could engage with a clear conscience. But when some seniors came to me and told me that Ambie's tormentor had arrived on campus as a freshman and asked what they should do about it, I have to confess that I told them to make sure to make his life as miserable as he had made Ambie's in high school. I guess it was the disgust that I had always had for bullies that made me want to see this guy get some of his own medicine.

By the time we graduated college, we found that this fellow who had in the past made life so miserable for my friend, Ambie, was quite a pleasant fellow after all. He had probably just gone along with what he saw his friends doing. In college, he quickly learned that what goes around sometimes will quickly come back around.

A Constant Reminder

I HAD JUST completed my two years of college and was getting ready to start the one year of internship when I received a message from one of my aunts that my biological father was coming to Jamaica from England and wanted to see his children. The aunt who relayed the message was the same one with whom our parents had initially left us with and who had refused to keep us because she wasn't getting any help from them to take care of us.

I had not kept in touch with Aunt Vena, but I later found out that she had found me through one of my brothers. Of all the people who have ever been in my life, this lady was perhaps my least favorite. She was someone who held only bad memories for me. I had wanted to have absolutely nothing to do with her.

She was the one who had turn over that pot of soup in the mud instead of allowing us to have some because she was angry with our parents. She was also the one who had beaten me so severely with the belt buckle end of a belt that it tore out the toenail completely from my left big toe.

My toenail never grew back properly after that. And for years, every time I would look at my deformed toenail, I would be reminded of the person who did that to me.

It was some sixty years later when one day, I was at home doing some work in my garage when I noticed that the deformed nail had suddenly fallen out. Beneath where the nail had been was nothing but flesh. But it was not raw like how it should have been from having just lost a nail, instead, it looked like healed flesh, sensitive to the touch but not hurting.

It was not long after that a new toenail began to grow in its place, and as it grew, instead of taking the shape of the old deformed nail, it resembled more the normal nail on my right foot.

This was so profound, and the symbolism was not lost on me. Sometimes, scars can be a reminder of a past hurts, but the Lord God and the love of a godly woman have helped me change the way I think about that scar. Scars don't have to be a reminder of a past wound—they can be a reminder that you are healed. When I look at my new toenail, I am no longer seeing a broken and disfigured part of my body. I see a toenail that is healed and whole again, just like my life.

I was to see this aunt again when my father came to Jamaica, and we went to see him at her house. I reminded her then about the pot of soup she had turned over in the mud instead of allowing us to have something to eat. Her only response was to wonder how it was that I was the only one who remembered it. She didn't deny it; she just marveled that after all those years, that memory had still stuck with me.

When I met her at her house, she was living by herself, and I couldn't help but wonder about what had happened to her husband and kids. I wouldn't see her again, and several years later, I heard that she had died.

An Unexpected Visitor

MY BIOLOGICAL FATHER'S name is John. It was very surprising one day in August 1973 when I got a message from my aunt that he was coming to visit from England. He and my mother, Amy, had left Jamaica in 1956, and we had not heard a thing from them since. And so here it was, 1973, some seventeen years later, and he was coming back to Jamaica and wanted to see us. Why?

One of my brothers and I talked about how we should respond to this since here was a man whom we did not know and had no relationship. All we knew was that he was the man who had fathered us, and for seventeen years, we did not know if he was dead or alive. We had grown up in orphanages and foster homes and were always conscious of the fact that we had no parents. So how should we respond to him now? And should we even bother to meet with him at all?

Maybe it was out of curiosity more than anything else, but we agreed that we would meet with him when he arrived. At the time, I had only vague memories of him, so I wasn't certain that I would remember him. I was only four years old when he and my mother left, and I was now twenty-one. I had no memory of what he looked like, and I, for one, could easily walk past him on the street and not know it was him. We agreed to meet him at his sister's house. When we got there, it was she who introduced him to us, saying, "This is your father."

The minute he opened his mouth, I remembered his voice. That was the voice I remembered being raised in anger against us and our mother when I was just a kid. The first time I ever became conscious of a feeling of hatred was the one night he had come home drunk and began beating up our mother. I remember that I felt absolute disgust and hatred for him. It was soon afterward that he left and went to England, so that had always been my most lasting memory of him.

Our initial meeting with our father could best be described as awkward. We didn't know what to say to him. We certainly did not feel comfortable calling him Dad since that was not who he was to us. He was a stranger with the same last name. We tried our best to make small talk with him, but as time went on, it because obvious that we would need to spend much time than we had at that time with the man who was our father in order to get to know him and for him to get to know us.

After our initial meeting with John, my brother and I agreed that John would spend a week with my brother in Kingston and then travel to the country to spend a week with me.

John arrived a week later, and during the course of the week as we talked, I noticed something strangely interesting. He spoke of "his wife" back in England and "his children" back in England. He never once referred to her as "your mother" or "your brothers and sisters," but always as "my wife" and "my children." It was as if we were total strangers to them and not flesh and blood.

In the course of our conversation, I found out that after they arrived in England, they had had six more children, two boys and four girls. What was interesting was that we in Jamaica didn't know anything about these new siblings in England, and apparently, they didn't know that we in Jamaica existed either.

I was never able to fully understand John's reason for coming to Jamaica in 1973. I don't know if he had just wanted to come back and test the waters to see where he stood with us or what! I never found out and he never said.

At one stage of his visit when I confronted him about the fact that they had left us and then had forgotten about us, his response was quite telling: "If I had not left, you would not be where you are today," he said. Say what?

It was then I realized that what he was doing was he wanted to take credit for the fact that unlike any other member of my family before me, I had gone to high school and college. In essence, what he was saying was that none of that would have been possible if he had stayed in Jamaica and we had grown up with him. And to a certain extent, he was absolutely correct.

John was completely illiterate, and the only thing he knew to do was manual labor. He didn't make any effort to send us to school for the few years we lived with him because he needed us to work on the plot of land he owned to help him with his farming. If he had remained in Jamaica, there was no doubt that was what I would probably have ended up doing as well. But for me, the fact that he thought that he should get some credit for the academic achievement of his children was outrageous. By the time he came back to Jamaica, the two girls, one of whom was only four months old when they left, were now getting ready to graduate from high school.

The other thing I realized was how many negative things he had to say about my brother with whom he had just spent a week. My loyalty was never going to be to my father, it was always going to be to my brothers and sisters whom they had left in Jamaica to basically fend for ourselves. So I checked with my brother to find out where all of this negativity was coming from. It was then that my brother informed me that he, too, had to listen to a litany of negativity that John was telling him about me.

We were perplexed as to why he should be doing this since there is no way that this man could dare to suggest that he knew either of us. He might be our biological father, but that didn't mean he knew us. It was then we both came to realize that what he was trying to do was trying to pit us against each other. We were having none of it, and so we devised a plan to deal with it.

When John came to Jamaica, he had brought some clothing for my brother and me. He also brought a cricket bat and some other things that I don't recall what they were at the moment. My brother and I decided that he would come down to the country to see me and bring all the gifts John had given him. John did not know he was coming and was very surprised the afternoon he turned up. We immediately confronted him about the negative things he had been saying to each of us about the other. He had no answer for his behavior. So we gave him back every item of gift he had given us, including the cricket bat, and told him that we wanted nothing from him, that he could leave, and we would be very happy if we never saw him again.

Soon after that, John left and went back to his sister's house and then back to England. I would not see or hear from him again for another five years.

Before John left Jamaica though, he was to do one last thing that I would later learn he very much came to regret. He decided to take my youngest sister back to England with him.

Same Old John

WHEN MY FATHER left Jamaica again in 1973, I did not hear a word from him again for nearly five years. Imagine my surprise then when in the summer of 1978, I got a phone call from him saying he was planning another visit to Jamaica. How he got hold of my phone number remains a mystery. Under normal circumstances, I have to admit I would have dismissed his call and told him that his coming to Jamaica was of no interest to me. But he caught me at a time when I was in a terrible bind.

Three years before, I had started working as a sales representative for Xerox Corporation in Kingston. I had done reasonably well, and within two years, I had purchased a Mercedes Benz, albeit a used one. Everything went well with my car for about eighteen months, and then suddenly, I began to have problems with the car. The straw that broke the camel's back was when I got in an accident through no fault of my own, and a part affecting the steering column broke and had to be replaced.

Much as I tried, I could not find the part to repair the problem anywhere on the island. I even tried getting the part from the United States but to no avail. It was while that was happening that I received that phone call from my father. As I spoke with him, it suddenly dawned on me that since the Mercedes I drove was specially designed to be driven on the left side of the road, similar to how the English drove, then maybe it would be easier to get the needed part in England.

I mentioned the problem I was having with the car, told him about the part I needed, and asked if he could get it and bring it for me. He assured me that he could and he would. That was probably the reason why when he arrived in Jamaica, my attitude toward him was much more positive than it had been the last time we met. He brought me the part and told me how happy he was to be able to do it. He said nothing about the cost, and to be honest, I didn't ask him.

John was not on the island but a few days before we realized that it was the same old John. He had to be the one dominating every conversation, and even though the man couldn't read or write, he somehow thought he knew everything.

There is no doubt that he was a pretty smart man. He was pretty knowledgeable about a lot of things. In the fifty-five years he lived in England, he didn't drive a car; he rode a motorcycle instead. I could only surmise that the reason was that it did not require much literacy to get a license to ride a bike as compared to obtaining a license to drive a car. I found out that for much of his time in England, he traveled throughout Britain and Europe helping to build roads and had gotten to where he was supervising a work crew. So I asked him how in the world was he able to help build roads when he couldn't read or write. He responded that he would look at the plans and memorize them. I believed him.

After a few days with us, it became obvious that we were not getting along and so he left. I found out later that part of the reason he had come back to Jamaica was to sell a piece of land he had in the little village where we were from. He did not tell us about his plan, and he didn't even offer to sell the property to any of his Jamaican children. I don't know if any of us would have had the funds to purchase it, but it would have been nice if he had even paid us the courtesy of asking if any of us wanted to buy it.

I also found out that was not the first time he had returned to the island since we last saw him in 1973. He had returned a few years after his initial visit accompanied by his eldest daughter of those born in England. He didn't let anyone know he was coming, and none of us had a chance to meet a sister whom we had never met. In fact, it wasn't until 1988 before I was to meet this particular sister. And so, my dad went back to England, but it wouldn't be long before I was to hear from them again.

Say What?

I USUALLY DIDN'T pay much attention to the mail when I lived in Jamaica. I didn't have any relatives on the island who were big letter writers, and I had no relatives living abroad who had ever written to me. So imagine my surprise when one day, not too long after my father returned to England, I received a letter in the mail, and the return address had my mother's name and address on it. Now understand this, I had not seen or heard from the lady in over twenty years, so why she would be writing me now was a complete mystery to me.

It was therefore with a sense of great anticipation that I opened the letter and read it. My jaw dropped in total shock. My mother's letter had nothing to do with wanting to find out how I was doing or how her two grandkids at the time were doing. Her letter also didn't mention anything about how our other siblings in England were doing. No, instead, in it, she set about berating me for what she said was my disgraceful treatment of her husband. Among the things she accused me of was taking advantage of him by having him bring me the part for my car and then not paying him for it. I was flabbergasted!

Apparently, John, being John, had gone back to England and had spun some tale to his wife to present us in the worst light possible, and she had swallowed his story hook, line, and sinker.

I chose not to respond to her lest I say something that was inappropriate for a son to say to his mother. It was one of those strange things with me. Even though I had not grown up with her, I had still somehow retained some affinity with her. I remember that even in school, with her far away in England, if someone made any derogatory remark about my mother, it would mean a fight. I believe that my sense of connection with her was based on the fact that when I was very young and before they had migrated to England, I had seen my father hit her, and it was then I had felt a sense of hatred for my father for daring to hit my mother.

It was obvious to me that that sense of connection that I still felt for her was not felt by her for me. Nowhere in her letter did she give the impression that here was a mother writing to her son. It was like we were both total strangers to each other. The fact that she was also doing what John had done the first time he had visited in 1973 when he kept referring to her as "his wife" rather than "your mother" was clear evidence to me that both of them were complicit in their abandonment of their kids in Jamaica and apparently felt no sorrow or sense of regret for what they had done to us. After I received that letter, I totally lost any sense that I had parents who were still alive. And it would be another ten years before I would hear from either John or Amy again.

Culture Shock

By 1987, I had been living in the United States for eight years. I had moved here with my family of two boys and one girl in 1979. To say the move meant a severe cultural shock for me would be an understatement.

I had visited the United States only two times before I moved here permanently. The first time was in 1969 when I flew into Miami and then on to Detroit, Michigan, on a Greyhound bus. The year before, I was part of a contingency of Jamaican schoolboy cadets who had been chosen to be part of an exchange program with cadets from Canada. During my stay in Canada, I had become friends with a young Canadian cadet named Dale Walker.

Dale had invited me back to visit with him and his family in 1969. It just so happened that in the summer of 1969, the Meads were all going back to England for a visit. Not wanting to leave me at home alone, they felt that I should go and visit my friend in Canada while they were away in England. They arranged for me to fly to Miami and then travel by Greyhound bus to Detroit where Dale's family would meet me, and we would then drive across the river to the city of Windsor where they lived.

My journey from Miami to Detroit was relatively uneventful. It took me a total of thirty-six hours, but the journey took me through some beautiful scenery as I traveled north. I was careful to make certain that I kept very close to the bus station when we stopped and to ask relevant questions to make sure I was always on the right bus for my journey to Detroit.

At the end of the summer, I reversed my journey, with the Walkers driving me to Detroit to get the bus for my journey to Miami. By that time, I had had enough of sitting on a bus and was ready to get back home.

The second time I visited the United States was in 1977. I won an all-expense paid weekend at the Doral Country Club in Miami. I was working for Xerox at the time and had done well enough as a sales representative that I was given that weekend in Miami for my performance. I had come on my own and was there from Friday until Monday before I returned home. Being in Miami all by myself meant that I stayed mainly around the resort. I didn't venture into town at all since I didn't know any of the places to go and I had no one to show me around.

And so it was about nine o'clock at night when I arrived in New York City for the very first time and in the United States for the third time. As the plane circled over the city, I remember looking out the window and marveling at the lights all over the city. I could see the highways from up in the air and wondered how in the world anyone could know where they were going in such a maze of roads.

I had arrived in New York to be reunited with my family who had left the island some two months before. I had left what was a very comfortable middle-class life in Jamaica and now found myself in a city where I had no idea what to expect.

Initially, my family and I had to live in a small studio apartment while I worked in a dry-cleaning shop, taking clothes from the washing machines and hanging them up on hangers. That was rock bottom for me. I had been used to traveling around Jamaica, driving a Mercedes, and making an excellent salary as a sales representative, and now here I was making minimum wage which was hardly enough to feed my family.

After two months in the dry-cleaning shop, a friend of my wife's family got me a job driving a truck for a plumbing supply company, making deliveries in Manhattan, the surrounding Burroughs, New Jersey, and Connecticut. I had no idea how I was going to manage that since I remembered the maze of roads that I had seen the night I landed and wondered how anyone knew how to navigate that. But I was determined to learn, since to me that was way better than been cooped up in a hot little shop all day, taking damp clothing out of a machine and hanging them up.

Nineteen seventy-nine was several years before the invention of the GPS, so whenever I had to go somewhere, I would write down detailed directions as to how to get there so I wouldn't get lost. I would also keep a record of all the directions of all the places I visited so that I could always consult it whenever I needed to.

I drove a truck for that company for seven years, and by the time I left, I no longer needed to ask for detailed directions. All I needed was the address because, over time, I had developed a built-in compass that allowed me to find places with relative ease. The maze of roads that had so intimidated me when I first saw them from the air had become as familiar to me as my backyard.

You Ought to Leave

MY LEAVING JAMAICA for the States was also due to some mitigating circumstances.

While working for Xerox, I had decided to further my education by attending classes at the University of the West Indies. Since I had graduated teachers' college, I now had the necessary qualification to get me into university. My goal was to pursue a degree in business so I could advance my career in the business sector in Jamaica.

I had started working at Xerox in 1975, some three years after Michael Manley had become prime minister of the island. His election had been a very popular one. He was widely supported by the vast majority of the people, and in 1972, when he was first elected, though I couldn't vote, I was an enthusiastic supporter of his. I was in my second year of college, and I remember staying up late and cheering loudly as his party won seat after seat in the nation's parliament. In its short history as an independent nation, no political party had been as enthusiastically lauded on its victory as Manley's party was in 1972.

By 1979, after seven years in power, I was among a large percentage of Jamaicans who had become totally disillusioned with Manley and his Democratic Socialist policies. In embracing socialism, he had alienated the United States and was pursuing a close relationship with Cuba's Fidel Castro. By that time, Jamaica was also fast losing its position as the most prosperous nation among the English-speaking Caribbean islands. There were severe scarcities for virtually everything, and people, particularly the middle class, were leaving the island in droves. In response, Manley had put a severe limit on the amount of money that could be taken out of the country, and this only served to heighten people's anxiety about what was happening.

Manley's response to so many people leaving the island was to give the impression that he really didn't care. "There are flights a day to Miami," he said, and many people took him up on it.

In addition, in order to foster a populist posture, Manley's party had begun to encourage and foster a sense of lack of discipline among their followers. Things that were once considered unacceptable were now being embraced and lauded. This indiscipline quickly began to take root in the society and particularly in the schools, and those who disagreed where labeled as reactionaries and unpatriotic.

While I was attending classes at the university, I had made no secret of my opposition to Manley and his policies, and as you can well imagine, this was not a popular position since the university was a hotbed of support for his policies. All the institutions that could be considered the bedrock of a nation democracy were now controlled by Manley's people, and in my mind, they were slowly moving the nation away from our democratic norms.

My brother, at the time, was working as a sports journalist for the leading newspaper on the island, and I would often accompany him to his meeting at the journalists' club, which was again another hot spot of support for Manley. I would often find myself in fierce arguments with many of these journalists. Being journalists, I had thought they would be more open-minded to listen to different points of view, but that was hardly the case. And so one day, after one of my visits, my brother told me that he had been advised by some of journalists to warn me to watch my back.

To me, this was no idle threat that could be ignored. The election that was held in 1977 was the most violent in the history of elections in Jamaica, and hundreds of people had lost their lives. So my brother's warning, together with the hostilities I was encountering on campus at the university, directly influenced my decision to pack up and leave Jamaica, and so I did.

That Was Dumb

WITHIN A YEAR of moving to New York, we had added another child, a daughter, to our family, which now consisted of two boys and two girls. While working as a truck driver, I had also gone back to school and had obtained a bachelor's as well as a master's degree.

Raising a family, working, and studying had been very challenging, but I was determined to set an example for my children. I would leave home very early each morning to get to the warehouse where I would pack up the day's deliveries and set out to complete the task so I could leave work by three thirty each day. My employer had supported my educational goals and had agreed that if I put in eight hours each day, then I could leave and go home after those eight hours. I had calculated that if I got to work by seven thirty each morning and avoided taking any lunch break, then I could leave work by three thirty. Leaving at that time allowed me to get home, have a bath, have something to eat, and then drive the seven or so miles to school. Classes were four days per week, usually from five to nine at night.

Because I had decided to pursue a degree in Computer Information Systems, it meant that I also had to spend a lot of Saturdays on campus, running programs on the computer. This was before personal computers were available. Fortunately, the college had a swimming pool to which we could take the kids for swimming. So while I was busy in the computer lab, Nicky and the kids could enjoy the pool.

As soon as I graduated with my bachelor's degree, I started working toward my master's. While the courses for the bachelor's had posed some challenges for me, the courses for the masters were even more so, and none more than a class in quantitative analysis that I chose to take during the summer.

I had no idea what the class entailed when I signed up for it. I soon found out that it was very mathematically based. Mathematics had never been one of my strong suits, and so when I took the midterm exam, I did very poorly. Undeterred, I had gotten some books and instructed myself in what I needed to know in order do better on the final exam.

I did so well on the final exam that the professor offered to give me an Incomplete and allowed me to take the class again in the fall without having to pay for it again. I was very grateful for his offer and gladly accepted. It meant that I would have a couple more weeks to familiarize myself with the class materials in order to do well in the class.

During the five years it took me to complete both degrees, I was usually the only black man in most of my classes. There were usually quite a few more black women, but rarely were there any black men at all. Imagine how pleasantly surprised I was when I started class in the fall and found out that the class was being taught by the same professor who had taught it during the summer, and in addition, there was another black man in the class with me. At the first opportunity, I introduced myself to my new classmate.

Taking classes at night often meant that you knew absolutely no one in those classes. In fact, during the five years I spent studying, I had only gotten to know two people well. Both had been a great help in propelling me toward graduating with my undergraduate degree with honors. So when I saw this other black man in the class, I went out of my way to befriend him. I told him that I had taken the class in the summer, had done poorly on my midterm, but had aced the final exam and the professor was allowing me to take the class again without having to pay for it.

When the time came for the midterm exam, I also told him that I had a copy of the midterm exam that I had taken in the summer in my briefcase and that I could give it to him so he would have an idea what to expect on the exam.

After the exam and after the professor had returned our paper, at the break, we were discussing how we had done. He told me that he had only gotten a C on the exam.

"So what did you get?" he asked. When I told him I had gotten a B, he looked at me with a look of incredulity on his face and with his voice dripping with sarcasm said, "You mean to tell me that you had a similar exam like this in the summer and you could only manage a B?"

Are you kidding me! Now it was my turn to look at him with incredulity.

Here he had only managed a C on the exam and only after I had shared a copy of the midterm with him, and now, he thought that that somehow gave him the right to berate me for getting a B? Without saying another word to him, I got up, walked away, and went back into the classroom. It was not time yet for the class to resume, and only the professor was there sitting at his desk.

When I walked in, he looked up and beckoned for me to come over and talk with him. He told me that since I had done well on the final exam in the summer and had gotten a B on the midterm test, he was going to give me a final grade of B for the course, and I did not need to complete the rest of the semester. I was ecstatic!

I quickly got my briefcase and walked out the door with a smile on my face, passed that black guy still sitting outside, and went home. The sad thing was that as I walked to my car, I was carrying in my briefcase a copy of the final exam from the summer that I could have given that guy if only he had not been such a pusillanimous jerk.

I Love New York! Nah

I HAVE OFTEN heard people exclaim how much they loved New York. That was not the case for me at all. There is no doubt that New York is a very interesting place indeed, and I guess that is why millions of people visit the city each year.

I lived in New York for nine years and never had the time to enjoy any of the interesting things about the city. I was up early in the morning to get to work, and my evenings and weekends were spent studying. In addition, I had a growing family that also demanded my attention.

I hated the traffic associated with the city. That was part of the reason why I had negotiated with my employer for me to start work early, so I could leave early in the afternoon, so I wouldn't have to get caught up in New York City's horrendous traffic jams. But no matter how much you planned to avoid it, it was inevitable that you were going to get caught up in bad traffic at some time or another.

Being from the warm climate of Jamaica, New York was too cold for me during the winter months. Having to constantly shovel snow during those months was no fun. In addition, driving a truck in the winter became even more hazardous. I never had any serious accidents, but there were several times when I came very close to it.

Having to negotiate your way through Manhattan traffic each day would often make me very agitated. And nothing would heighten that agitation more than having to deal with New York cops. I had many encounters with them, and I remember that my response was always one of belligerence and anger. Looking back, I am very surprised that I was not seriously harmed by one of them because when I was stopped for any traffic violation; my immediate response was to react with anger.

New York was also too crowded. I was used to open spaces and being able to sit outside your house with your family. In New York, the houses were all bunched up together, and you spent virtually all your time indoors. I hated that.

The one thing I did really like about the city was the number of colleges and universities that were in close proximity to where I lived. I was determined to get as good an education as I possibly could. So as soon as I was able, I registered for college and completed an undergraduate degree with honors and a masters' degree also with honors.

I thought that those two degrees were going to open up opportunities for me to improve the financial situation for me and my family. And so I got busy sending out résumés to companies all over the city. I got very few responses and even fewer interviews. None of my interviews panned out. It was as if they liked my qualifications, but when I turned up for the interview, suddenly, I wasn't the right person.

And so it happened that one day, while riding the train back home from an interview and frustrated from not being able to land a well-paying job, I struck up a conversation with a gentleman seated next to me.

He said something very interesting to me during the course of our conversation. He said that they needed a lot more black educators like myself and suggested that I try teaching in the public school.

Frankly, teaching in an American public school was something I had vowed I would never do. I had read about the level of indiscipline that existed in these schools, and I wanted to have nothing to do with that. I had taught in Jamaica for three years, and while there was always some indiscipline in the schools, it was nowhere near what I had heard about American schools.

In Jamaica, when a teacher turned up for class, the students would stand, would be greeted by the teacher, would respond by saying "Good morning, sir" or "Good morning, miss" before they were invited by the teacher to sit. During the course of the class, students would raise their hands to ask or answer a question and stand before doing so. These were quaint little things that I understood were not done in American schools.

There was also another aspect to American school that influenced my disinterest in becoming a teacher. Racism has always been a part of American society. It is an ingrained part of American culture. I was used to teaching kids who were mostly black and who respected their teachers. I did not feel that that would be the case in the classrooms in American.

And so, it was with those kinds of thoughts in mind that I sought a teaching position in a community college, rather than in a public school. I was only able to get a part-time position, and while it paid well, I was only able to work eight hours per week.

I taught an adult education class at the community college in the Bronx for one year. Then, in 1988, I packed up my family and moved to Florida.

We're Moving to the Sunshine State

THE INITIAL DECISION to move to Florida was not mine. Even though New York was not my favorite place to live, I had more or less determined that I would stick with it especially for the sake of my kids. My oldest son was in a class for gifted kids and was doing very well. In addition, all four of my children were learning to play the piano, and I thought that was an ability that I wanted them to continue to develop. They had an excellent teacher whom they loved, and each year, he would have a recital where he allowed the kids to showcase what they had learned. So I had more or less decided that New York was where we were going to be.

And then in the summer of 1988, Nicky decided that she wanted to go to Florida to visit her brother who had moved to Florida the year before. That was fine with me, and so she took our youngest daughter and flew to Florida. I remained in New York because I had to teach during the summer.

About a week after she left for Florida, Nicky called me to say that she had decided that she was not coming back to New York, and I was to pack up the other children and move down. I was very hesitant about this, but she assured me that she had already gotten a job, had rented an apartment, and would have everything ready for us to come. I packed up the other three children and send them down as unaccompanied minors by plane. I still had a few weeks to go before the summer term ended and then I planned to drive down to be with them.

It took me two days to make the journey by car from New York to Riviera Beach, Florida. When I arrived, I found out that nothing Nicky had told me was true. She did not have a job or an apartment, and instead, we would have to stay with her brother, his wife, and their three kids. I was not happy. The little money I had, I used it to quickly find us a suitable place to live.

Despite the fact that I didn't have a full-time, well-paying job in New York, I had felt that it was only a matter of time before I would find something suitable that would allow me to take care of my family. Now here I was in a new state without a job or a place of our own to live. Nicky explained that when she first arrived in Florida, the weather reminded her so much of Jamaica that she thought it would be good for us to move there. She felt that I probably would not be too open to the idea, so she painted the best picture possible in order to get me to come.

I had to quickly set about finding a job and was able to find a part-time position at Palm Beach Community College, teaching math in the Center for Personalized Instruction.

Despite the fact that I ended up in Florida by what could at best be called deceptive means, after a while, I was glad to be out of that cold and crowded city of New York.

An Unexpected Call

ONE SATURDAY AFTERNOON, the summer before moving to Florida, I was at home in my apartment when I got a phone call from my brother who had recently moved to New York from Jamaica.

This was the time before caller ID, so when the phone rang, you would not know who was on the other end until you answered it. The caller identified himself as my brother, and he told me that he was up in Spring Valley visiting one of our father's sisters.

After we chatted for a while, he suddenly said, "There is someone here who wants to speak to you."

Before I could say anything, a lady's voice came over the phone. "Hello, do you know who this is?"

She spoke with what I recognized as a Jamaican trying to speak with an English accent, but I had no idea who the person was, and so I said, "No."

"It's your mother" was the response. I immediately hung up the phone.

At that time, as far as I was concerned, my mother was dead. From the time she left us in Jamaica some thirty-one years ago, I had only heard from her once, and that was when that she had written me that letter berating me for being rude to her husband and not paying him for the car part he had brought for me. I had not responded to her letter and had figured that I would never hear from or see her again. And now here was this woman on the phone saying, "This is your mother." I didn't have a mother. She was dead to me.

Not too long after I had hung up the phone, it rang again. It was my brother again. I was very upset with him for putting me in the position he did by not telling me who wanted to speak to me before he put her on the phone. He apologized and tried to convince me that despite what had happened in the past, I should take the opportunity to come and see our mother. According to him, she was also very much wanted to meet her grandkids.

Apparently, both parents had come to New York to visit my father's sister, and they were able to get in touch with my brother whom they invited up to Spring Valley to see them. It was while visiting that they asked if he knew how to get in touch with me since they had heard that I had moved to New York from Jamaica some eight years previously. My brother was the only relative of mine that had my phone number, and so he called thinking that I would be open to speaking to my mother. I wasn't!

Before my brother called back, I had told Nicky that there was a lady on the phone claiming to be my mother and I had hung up on her. After the second phone call with my brother, Nicky suggested we go so that the kids could meet their grandparents.

Now up to this point, I had never told my children anything about my past or about my parents, and so they were of the opinion that the Meads were their only grandparents. The Meads had visited us in New York from England three years before, and their only daughter had also come and spent time with us one summer. So now here I was having to explain to them why they were only now hearing about my real parents and their grandparents for the very first time.

I decided to go visit my parents in Spring Valley. The visit with my parents was an awkward one. When I first arrived at my aunt's house, I was very reluctant to go in to see my parents. My brother and my aunt were the ones who came and encouraged me to come in the house. I did not know what to expect in meeting my mother. I had no idea what she looked like and so it was like I was going to meet a stranger for the very first time.

I walked into the room and looked into the face of a stranger who looked at me and said, "Hello, Earl." We hugged.

During the course of our visit, my parents went on as if nothing had happened in the past, and they were so happy to see us and meet the grandkids. I tried to be as pleasant as I could, but when we left to go home that afternoon, the two people we had just met were still strangers to me.

Dad Is Gone

I WAS IN my first month working at the community college in Florida when I got a phone call from Mrs. Mead in England, "Earl, Dad is gone."

I could not believe it. He was only sixty-four years old and was dead? How could that be? I remembered that for many days after that, all I could do was cry when I thought of it.

I had lost the most important man to have ever come into my life. I remember while I was living in New York and going to college that one of the things that kept me going was wanting the Meads to be proud of me. I wanted them to know that their efforts on me had not been in vain, that I was succeeding at making something positive of myself. I remember writing Mr. Mead a letter in frustration at not being able to land a good -paying job, so I could tell him how well I was doing and for him to be proud of me. He quickly wrote me back to remind me that I had not let them down and how proud they were of me. And now he was gone. This man, who had been this colossus, this giant, in my life was now gone. I was heartbroken. I truly loved the man. He was such an example to me of how a man who called himself a Christian ought to behave. He was the man I was wanting to pattern my life after. And now he was gone.

They say the good die young, and as I thought of Mr. Mead, I thought that here was a man who had absolutely no reason to and yet he took me into his family and raised me as one of his own, and now at only sixty-four, he had died. My biological father who had abandoned me and my brothers and sisters and had contributed absolutely nothing to our lives, he would live to the ripe old age of eighty-eight before he died. Life just isn't fair.

I flew to England for the funeral of the man I had come to regard as my dad. It was the first time that I was seeing some of the other Mead children since they left Jamaica in 1970. I had seen the only girl in the family when she had come and spent a few days with us in New York. All the others were now married and some had children of their own. And apart from two of them, all were teachers like myself.

I had not been in touch with any of the Mead children since they left Jamaica, and so we spent the time I was in England catching up on what had been happening in each of our lives. It was on that visit that, for some inexplicable reason, one of the sons, Stephen, and I began to develop a very close relationship. To Stephen, I was not just someone who had once lived with his family, I was his brother. It didn't matter that I was black and he was white. We were brothers, and from that time onward, that was what we remained.

Stephen was one of those rare people who had struggled through school because no one recognized that he had a learning disability, but it turned out that he was a relative genius when it came to computers. Stephen worked in computers until he and the family moved to Australia where he went into ministry.

I was to visit Stephen and his family in England many times before he moved to Australia and developed a very close relationship with his kids, especially Barney and Emily whom we all affectionately refer to as M&M! Steve, as I called him, lived in the seaside town of Bognor Regis, and during my visits, it was my responsibility and great joy, really, to go and get the kids from school. I thought it must have been a funny scene outside that school when they would ask me who I was there to pick up. I would be asked that since I was the only black person around, and then out the door would run Barney and little Emily screaming, "Uncle Earl, Uncle Earl" as they ran into my arms. I am sure that turned a head or two. Then off we would go walking home with a little overactive white boy on one hand and an adorable little redheaded girl on the other with this big black man in between them. It was funny and so much fun for me.

Emily would ask me all sorts of question about America. When I told her I lived in Florida, she made me promise that when she comes to visit, I would take her to Disney. I wasn't sure when she would get to America, but I promised.

I Need Your Help

AFTER STEVE AND his family moved to Australia in 2003, our contacts became few and far between. It was soon after that I got a computer and could Skype, and we were able to connect with each other again. On one of our Skyping sessions, he mentioned to that he needed my help. I was happy to do anything I could for my brother.

Apparently, Emily, who had by now grown into an adorable young woman, had just announced that she wanted to go to America to visit her uncle. Steve was all for her coming since he knew how close Emily and I have always been. And so he was wondering if I would spend some time talking with her and maybe be able to give her some advice. He didn't give very much detail except to say that he was very concerned about her relationship with one particular boy whom he thought was not in her best interest. Of course, I said I would do everything I could, but I didn't know if she was more likely to listen to me than her dad.

When Emily arrived in Florida, I was amazed at how beautiful my little M&M had become. I was seeing her for the first time in nearly twenty years, but there was no missing that effervescent personality. The very first thing she reminded me of when she arrived was my promise to take her to Disney. And so I immediately set about making plans to take her to Disney and was able to keep the promise I had made to that adorable little four-year-old all those many years ago.

While trying not to appear to be prying into her private affairs, Emily and I sat down one day and had a good long chat. I mentioned about her dad's concerns and wondered what was it she wanted to do with her life. She appeared not to be particular certain about what direction her life was going in, and that was part of her reason for coming to America to visit so she could get some fresh perspective. Her visit with us was so wonderful that we hated when she had to leave.

Not long after she returned to Australia, her dad called to say that Emily had returned refreshed and a lot more focused. She had ended her relationship with that particular guy and was dating a Christian young man who had his full approval. Three years later, my wife and I would fly to Australia to attend Emily's wedding to that young man. Emily was insistent that her uncle from America be there for the wedding, and I was not going to disappoint her.

Since I hadn't seen Steve in over twenty years, Emily had decided that she would not tell her dad that I was coming for the wedding and so it would be a big surprise when I turned up. For more than six months, we planned and plotted as we shared plans with each other. She had to let her mother in on the plans however, since she would have to make the necessary arrangements for us to stay with them. During the course of the six months, Emily told me that her dad would often ask her if she had invited me to the wedding. Her response to him was that she had, but I was not certain I would be able to make it. He apparently had left it at that.

When Mary and I flew in to Brisbane, Emily had secretly arranged for us to be picked up the airport and driven back to her dad's house where we would surprise him. We got picked up and drove back to his house, only to find out he was not there. As we sat around waiting, the phone rang. It was Steve saying he was at his son Joe's house and would be there for a while. So we decided to drive over, still intending to surprise him with my visit.

When we arrived at Joe's house, Emily and her mom decided that they would go in first and try and distract Steve and I would then walk in and greet him. Everything seemed to be going according to plan until I walked in and before I could say anything, Steve who was sitting with his back to me, without even turning around, said, "Oh hi, Earl."

What?

"How did you know I was here?" I asked.

"Easy," he said. "I got a phone call from Nicole a few minutes ago wanting to know if her dad had arrived yet."

You are kidding me! After months of planning to surprise him, it turned out not to be the surprise I had hoped it would be after all, as my daughter Nicole had unknowingly spilled the beans

Steve had also apparently figured out that something was afoot. For one thing, he said, his wife was busy getting the spare room ready, and most importantly, he didn't think that I would just not turn up for M&M's wedding. He was right about that.

One of the saddest days of my life was in 2020, in the middle of a worldwide pandemic, Emily called me to tell me that her dad and my brother had died. With all the travel restrictions in place, it was impossible for us to travel to Australia for Steve's funeral. I will miss him, but it is good to know that his was a life well lived, and we will certainly see each other again.

Being at the Right Place

BEFORE I MOVED to Florida in 1988, I was exploring the possibility of going to law school. I had taken the LSAT and, based on my results, had applied to several schools. By the time I left for Florida, I had been accepted into two law schools, both of which were up north.

In my first year in Florida, since I only had a part-time position teaching in the community college, I decided I would try again to get into a law school here in the state.

By the time the new school year came around in 1989, I was accepted at Nova Southeastern University School of Law. But I now faced a dilemma. A full-time position as a business instructor had also opened up on the college's north campus for which I had applied and was informed that I was the one chosen to fill the position. What was I to do?

I had developed a very strong interest in the law from watching the Iran-Contra Affair hearings on television. I was mesmerized by the questions and the different aspects of the law that was involved. So I had decided then and there that I was going to be a lawyer. But by now, I had moved to a new state and still had a young and growing family to support. If I chose to go to law school, it would mean having to borrow funds to pay for schooling, and I was already carrying some student loans from my graduate degree. I decided that I would forego law school and take the full-time instructor's position at the college.

I would have to teach in that position for three years before I could be tenured. In those three years, I was asked to teach a variety of subjects in the business department, which I gladly did. It was all part of a learning process for me and allowed me to expand my knowledge. I also thought that it would be a great asset to the college to show that I had the ability and flexibility to teach in a variety of areas.

And so, when 1992 came around, I was fully expecting to be offered tenure by the college. It didn't happen. As it happened, 1992 was not a good year economically, and all around the state, funds were being cut for education. It meant that the college had to cut staff, and the first to go would be those without tenure. Unfortunately, I was one of those. To say I was disappointed would be an understatement. I felt that I had shown myself to be a versatile instructor who could masterfully teach in a variety of areas in the business department, but it was to no avail. Once again, I found myself without a job and, due to the economic situation, not certain where to look to find a suitable replacement.

It was while watching television one night that I saw a report that a nearby county was looking to hire more minority teachers. I had no idea where that county was, and so one day, I got in my car and got on I-95 heading north, hoping to see some indicator that would lead me to where this county was—this was well before Google Maps was available in the palm of your hand.

I must have traveled for nearly an hour before I realized that I was not seeing anything that was leading me to where I wanted to go. I noticed that I was coming up to an exit marked Orange Avenue. I got off and went east until I came to a gas station. I didn't know what county I had driven to, but I was certain there had to be a school board building nearby where I could get some information. And so, I walked into the gas station and asked a gentleman if he could direct me to the school board. He indicated that all I needed to do was go to the next light, turn left, and the school board building would be on my right. Although I had come to a totally different county from the one I had initially set out to get to, I had driven to within a few hundred feet of the school board and didn't know it.

I told the lady who greeted me at the front desk why I was there, and right away, she took me in to see the person in charge of personnel. It was almost as if he had been waiting for me to come. After a short conversation to find out about my educational background, he sent me about a mile away to a magnet school to speak to the principal about the possibility of a teaching position. Mark you, by this time, I had been teaching in America for five years, but all of those years I had been teaching adults. Teaching in a public school was still not what I wanted to do, but with four young children and no job, I was desperate.

I met with the principal, Dr. Elizabeth Lambertson, at the magnet school, and after a long conversation, she took me on her golf cart for a tour around the campus. The magnet school consisted of both middle and high schools. It was considered to be the premier school in the county and catered only to the smartest students. Parents would register their kids at birth in order to ensure them a place in the school at the appropriate time.

After asking some questions about how I would approach teaching in a particular scenario, the principal offered me a position teaching computer science to grade six students. Grade six was where middle school started, and I was now going to be teaching ten- and eleven-year-old kids computer science.

And so, during the summer of 1992, our young family moved to St. Lucie County, and at the beginning of the 1992–1993 school year, I began my new career as a middle school teacher. It was not something I was looking forward to, but due to the circumstances, I had no choice.

Here We Go Again

TEACHING MIDDLE SCHOOL kids might not have been my first choice, but I jumped in with full commitment from day one. There were a whole new set of dynamics in place now that I was teaching in the public school. The major one being that I had to be certified in the area in which I was teaching. Even though I had an undergraduate degree in computer systems, it still meant that I would have to go back to college to take additional courses in order to become a certified teacher in that subject. Besides, by the time I was being asked to teach this subject, nearly ten years had passed since I had graduated with my degree, and computer technology was now way ahead of what I knew when I graduated. Each day, I would come to school knowing that I didn't have mastery of the subject I was teaching, and I didn't.

Years later, by the time I had finished my career as a teacher, I figured I had taught multiple thousands of students. If anyone was to ask me to name any of the students I had taught in all those years, I wouldn't be able to, except for one. His name was Anthony Torres, and he was a student in my computer science class that first year I started teaching in a public school.

Anthony was, without doubt, the smartest kid I had ever taught. But it was not just his smarts that made him memorable all these many years later. No, I remembered him mainly for the way he conducted himself in my class that first year. Each day, as I tried my best to understand the new terms and skills necessary to teach the subject,

I was grateful that the students in the class knew even less that I did about the subject, all except Anthony. The boy was a virtual genius who got straight As in all his subjects. He knew a lot more than I ever did and could easily have done a better job teaching the class than I felt I was doing.

Most middle school students, if given an opportunity to show up the teacher in front of their class, would not hesitate to grab hold of such an opportunity. But not young Mr. Torres! Anthony sat at the back of the class, quietly listening but never asking any questions. Then at the end of the class, when all the other kids were gone, he would quietly walk up to my desk and point out certain important facts that I had missed or didn't know. And so, it went on for the entire year: Anthony Torres was my teacher, and not once did he let on to the other students what he was doing to help me. For that, I will always be grateful to him, and that is why after all these years and having had thousands of students go through my classrooms, there is still only one name that I will always remember well and that is Anthony Torres.

It was as I was struggling through teaching my first year in public school that I decided that in order to update my knowledge in computer technology, I would get certified as a teacher of computer science. I would have three years to get that done before I could be considered for a professional contract or as a tenured teacher.

Nearing the end of my first year at the school, the principal called me in to say that there was going to be some changes at the school, and my position teaching computer science was going to be eliminated, so there was not going to be a position for me in the new school year. *Oh boy*, I thought, *here we go again*. I thanked her for having given me the opportunity in the first place and left her office.

As I walked back to my classroom, I thought that since I hadn't really wanted to teach in the public school in the first place, that I would try finding a position with the nearby community college. But they had no openings for my qualifications, and so as the school year wound down, I was left wondering again what I was going to do. Thankfully, I didn't have to wait long.

About a week before the school year ended, I was again called into the principal's office. One of the sixth-grade social studies teachers had indicated that he would not be returning for the coming school year and she was offering me the position if I wanted it. Did I? I grabbed it with both hands. I went home for the summer break at least with the assurance that I would still have a job when the new school year came around. It also meant that now I would also have to get certified as a social studies teacher.

It was my experience of being let go by the community college and then almost not having a job after a year teaching at the magnet school that spurred me on to further my education. I thought that if I was going to give myself more options, I needed to get a doctoral degree, and so in November 1994, I started classes at Nova Southeastern University in Fort Lauderdale.

I Don't Need This

APART FROM DOING my classes for the doctoral degree, I also had to take other classes to be certified in the subject areas I was teaching. It meant that I was extremely busy. After two years teaching at the magnet school, the principal who hired me was replaced and went to work out of the school board offices. She was now the person in charge of making sure that all teachers complete all the necessary college courses they needed to be certified in their areas of teaching. I had worked extremely hard to complete the courses that I needed to be certified as a teacher of computer science and social studies. Being certified in social studies became the most important since that was the subject that I was currently teaching.

Imagine my surprise when my former principal called me to the school board and informed me that I was missing one course for my certification. I assured her that I had already done that course. She didn't believe me and insisted that unless I had the course completed by the end of the semester, I would no longer have a job. I was not pleased.

By the time she had informed me of this, the registration for all classes at the community college had already closed. I didn't see how I was going to be able to get into the class that I needed. Nevertheless, I went to the college and spoke to the professor who taught the course to find out if there was any possibility of me getting into his class even though the registration period had passed and the class had already begun. He told me that I would have to make a special application that would include a cover letter accompanied by a copy of my résumé. Why he needed those things he didn't say, and I didn't ask. I just made sure I got them to him as quickly as I could.

He agreed to let me do the class on my own as long as I submitted all the required written papers to him at the times designated. All this I had do while also making sure that all the work necessary for my doctoral degree was being done and handed in on time as well.

At the end of the semester, I quickly got a copy of my grade from the registrar at the college and took it to the school board and made sure I personally handed it to my former principal who had been adamant that I still needed that course and failure to complete it would mean I would be without a job.

When I arrived home after that visit, I received an envelope in the mail from the Commissioner of Education in Tallahassee. In it was the certificate showing that I was certified to teach both computer science and social studies in the State of Florida. I immediately made a copy and headed back to the school board office. I went in and, without saying a word, handed my former principal a copy of the certificate from the State of Florida that showed that I was *already* a certified teacher of computer science and social studies.

I wanted her to see that there was no way that the state would have sent me the certificate if I had not already completed the course she had insisted that I had to take. I had spent all that time, all that effort, and all the expenses on something that I didn't need, and it was just because she had not done her due diligence before she came to threaten me with losing my job. As you can well imagine, I was not very happy with what she had put me through.

Several weeks later, my former principal came and apologized profusely for her mistake. She assured me that it was not done deliberately. I assured her that I had put it all behind me and was moving on.

The Family Comes to Visit

IT WAS IN the middle of all the drama going on with my job, studying for the certification and my doctorate that I received a phone call from my parents that they wanted to come and visit me in Florida. They weren't coming alone either. They were bringing two of their daughters, Yvonne and Carol, and a son, Jeff, of those born in England with them. They also said that their other son, Neville, would also be coming, but he would be arriving a few days after they got here. We did not have a big house. It was only a three-bedroom, two-bathroom house which already had seven people living in it. Where were we going to find room for six more people? Despite that, I told them that it would be all right to come, and so the trip was planned for the summer of 1995.

In the years since I had met with them in 1987 in Spring Valley, New York, I had had to visit England at least twice for the funeral of Mr. Mead and then Mrs. Mead. It was while in England for Mrs. Mead's funeral that I decided to go and visit my parents and get to know the brothers and sisters I had never met. Of their six additional children, I had met only two on my visit. While it did ease the tension between me and my parents somewhat, it didn't totally eliminate it. So I had returned to Florida with no expectation of ever seeing or hearing from them again.

As the time for my parents' visit approached, one my brothers of those born in Jamaica, Barry, who was at the time living in New York, decided that he would come down to Florida to see them also.

My oldest sister, Joan, who was also born in Jamaica, also decided that she would come, as did my parents' oldest grandson, Glenmore, who was living in California at the time. At one point during their visit, we had a total of sixteen people staying in our little house. How we all fit, I don't have a clue, but there we all were.

The oldest son from England, Neville, came and stayed for only two days before he left. My parents stayed for nearly three weeks. After the first week, things really got tight with me financially. I was spending all the money I had to buy food to feed everyone. I think my father saw that my finances were running low, and he stepped in to help. But despite the fact that everyone was eating three meals a day and using my car to go back and forth, no one else was offering to help with any of the cost in any way and my father was livid. In no uncertain terms, he told them that they needed to do something to help with the additional expenses their visit caused. Even so, they never provided any assistance, and after an additional two weeks, they all left for Jamaica to continue their vacation.

The three weeks they spent with us really aggravated and annoyed my two oldest daughters, Nicole and Alicia. They felt that the kids from England were insensitive and lazy and only wanted to use them as servants to meet their needs. To be honest, during the course of their visit, I was also very busy with my doctoral studies, and so I didn't have much time to pay attention to what was going on. It was many years later that Neville told me the reason he left was because I was always so busy studying. He felt that it was insulting that he had come all the way from England to visit and I couldn't do him the courtesy of spending time with him. Looking back, I could understand why he felt that way. But my studies had me on a tight schedule, and I had to have my work handed in at the designated times or I would fail my class, and failure of even one class meant that I would be kicked out of the doctoral program.

Despite the hiccups, I had thought that the visit with my family had been worthwhile. For one thing, I had gotten to meet the youngest sister of the family, Carol, for the very first time, and in the course of a conversation I had with her, I mentioned that it was a pity we hadn't grown up together because I was sure I would have enjoyed walking her to school and coming to pick her up afterward.

About two weeks after their visit, I received a letter in the mail, and it was from Carol, one of the sisters born in England. Imagine my shock when I opened it and found that she was writing to tell me about all that was wrong in my household, including the fact that my marriage to Nicky was falling apart and I didn't even see it. She went on to tell me that I was lying to her when I told her I would have walked her to school if we had grown up together since I had not even bothered to get in touch with her since she left. Talk about being shocked. It was like reliving that letter her mother had written to me in Jamaica, cussing me out for disrespecting her husband.

How is it that these people felt so compelled to tell me off with no compunction? I thought. Where did she get the audacity to write to tell me about what was wrong in my house after only knowing me for two weeks? It was amazing to me. Like the letter I had received from my mother way back in 1978, I chose not to respond. It was further evidence to me that there was absolutely no hope of there ever being any reconciliation between those of us born in Jamaica and those siblings born in England. At the time, I had lived for more than forty years without having anything to do with them and I was not now going to let it become a major concern of mine.

See Nothing, Hear Nothing

My LITTLE SISTER's unsolicited observation about my marriage to Nicky was falling apart, and I did not even seem to realize it turned out to be true. At the time she wrote the letter, I was blissfully unaware of the rot that had crept into our marriage and was slowly destroying it.

To say I kept myself busy during those years would not be stretching the truth. For example, take my activities with the church I attended: I was there for Sunday service, on Monday for choir practice, Tuesday for school of the Holy Spirit, Wednesday for midweek service, Friday for Friday night service, Saturday for public outreach in the community, and back on Sunday for Sunday service. And that was how my week went. Thursday was the only night I had to myself, and it was the night of the week that I spent doing my work for my doctoral studies. In addition, I was teaching gifted kids who required more than just your average attention, so I always made sure that all my lesson plans were ready to go weeks in advance.

By this time, my oldest son had left and was on his own. Our other four children were still living at home. Our two oldest girls attended the magnet school where I taught and traveled with me every day to and from school. I really don't know what my thinking was about at the time, except that I thought that everything I was doing was to show that I was being the best father and husband possible. I considered myself a very loving and doting father who was strict regarding certain things, one of which was that I would never allow the kids to be rude to their mother. To that end, they knew that I would never entertain any complaints from them about Nicky, so they never did.

During the summer months when I had some time, I would often go with a friend of mine to Jamaica to do mission work. I would always go alone since it would have been impossible for Nicky and I both to go. When I went to Jamaica during the summer, Nicky would stay behind to take care of the kids. It was after my return from a mission trip to Jamaica in the summer of 1995 that all hell broke loose in my home and in my marriage, and life as I knew it was changed forever.

You've Got to Be Kidding

I JUST WALKED through the door that Monday night after driving up from Belle Glade when the phone rang. I had spent the previous week on a mission trip to Jamaica where I preached at about five venues and was to speak at a sixth. However, I was so tired that the group left and went without me because I had fallen asleep. Overall, the group leader had considered it a successful trip, considering all we were able to do and accomplish.

We had flown into Miami and then driven by bus to Belle Glade where I had parked my car. From Belle Glade to my house was about an hour-and-a-half drive, and despite the fact that I was very tired, I was looking forward to getting home, seeing my family, and getting some rest.

The last thing I wanted when I walked through the door of my house that night at about nine o'clock was to get a telephone call asking me to leave my house again to meet someone. And that is exactly what that phone call was about. It was the pastor of our church, and when I answered, he told me that it was very important that I come immediately to the church to see him. I told him that I would and hung up. It was after I hung up that I realized that only the children were home. I ask where their mother was, and none of them knew. I told them to lock the door behind me and set out for the church about four miles away.

I had no idea what the pastor wanted to see me about, and as I drove to the church, I was not worried or concerned about any-

94

thing. Even the fact that my wife was not home with the kids did not really bother me that much as I was sure that she would have a viable explanation. I pulled into the church parking lot, got out of the car, and headed to the pastor's office. I was shocked when I walked in to the office to find Nicky sitting there with our pastor. I immediately became concerned.

The pastor greeted me very warmly and asked about my trip to Jamaica. I hurriedly answered his question, all the while wondering what this was all about. Nicky just sat there very quietly and saying nothing, but I also noticed that she didn't look at me at all. She just kept looking down on the ground in front of her.

Finally, the pastor addressed me. "Earl, all of us make mistakes, and all of us have needed to be forgiven at one time or another in our life."

Fine, I thought, *but what does that have to do with me?*

It was then that he dropped the bomb.

"Earl," he said, "your wife has come to me to confess that she has been having an affair and she is very sorry that it happened and she wanted to start making things right."

Say what?

To say I was shocked would be the understatement of the year. Say what! I didn't believe it! In fact, I was so certain that the pastor was mistaken that I looked at him and said, "Pastor, if it wasn't you saying this to me, I would punch you in the face."

He just looked at me and continued, "Your wife is here tonight to ask for your forgiveness and for you both to move forward together."

I didn't know what to say. I was still in shock and finally found myself saying, "Well, I guess I have to forgive her since Christ has forgiven me."

The pastor smiled, got up, and gave us both a hug, and we left his office in total silence.

I drove my car behind her car all the way home in total shock. I was still trying to process what I had just heard, and I had no idea how I was going to deal with it. The one thing I knew was that there was no way I was going to tell the kids about this since I didn't want them to think in any way negative about their mother.

We got home, got in the house, and went to bed without saying a word to each other. I don't know if she was able to sleep that night, all I know was that sleep didn't come to me at all no matter how tired I was feeling. My mind was going at a hundred miles an hour. How did this happen? When? Who has she been with? All these and a thousand other questions were coursing through my mind as I lay there in total torment.

The thing I remembered well about that night also was that I didn't cry. I knew that something had been lost, but I got up the following morning and began to blame myself for what had happened. I was too busy. Maybe I had neglected her, and on and on, it went. I remember saying to her that I would stop preaching altogether until we fix our marriage, and to that end, I got all my sermon notes and threw them in the garbage. In my mind, I could not be out saying I am doing ministry when my marriage was falling apart. I needed to fix it first before I could go back to any form of ministry.

Despite my best resolutions, I still found myself tormented by what the pastor told me. At the meeting, she had told the pastor that she had broken off the relationship with the guys and was going to do all she can to make the marriage work. The question that I just couldn't get rid of though was who was the guy? And so finally, I said to her, "Please explain to me how this happened."

Her answer shocked me even more than the prior revelation.

"You won't be able to handle it," she said, "so I am not going to tell you anything."

It was right then I realized that things were never going to be the same again. I thought of divorce at the time, but my understanding of scripture was so tied up with the law that I had somehow conflated my marriage with my Christianity. I thought that if I divorced her, I would lose my salvation. As dumb as that sounds, that was how I thought at the time. It was obvious from the answer she gave me that she had lied to the pastor when she said she was going to do everything she could to make the marriage work. From that day on, I don't remember any such effort on her part. And so I settled in to living an unfulfilled life in a broken marriage for the rest of my life.

Tormented

CALL IT PRIDE or ego, but I was never able to get the affair out of my mind. Nicky was adamant that she was not going to share any information with me, and so I set about on my own to find out what had happened.

By piecing little tidbits of information together, I was able to find out about a particular office building that she had been visiting. When I went there, I found out that it was the office of an insurance agent. The agent's name was on the marquee in front of the building, and so I went in, told his secretary my name, and that I was there to see him. He told her to tell me to wait and he would see me soon. I sat in that waiting area for nearly an hour before he asked me to come into his office. I told him who I was and that I was there to find out what was going on between him and my wife. He told me everything, including the fact that he was married and had kids. He said that Nicky just turned up at his office and waited to see him, and when they were alone, one thing led to another. This affair had been going on for some time, he said.

He also mentioned that he had been afraid to ever run into me because Nicky had told him that I was a very violent man and probably would kill him if I found out about their affair. We talked for about an hour during which he told me a whole myriad of things, much of which I have chosen to forget.

He did give me the very strong impression though that it was Nicky who had been pursuing him and not him pursuing her. He even mentioned that she had wanted him to run away with her and go to Jamaica. I left that guy's office that day sad but still angry. I had found out what I wanted to know, but it still didn't lift the sense of torment I had in my soul.

I made it a point to let Nicky know that I had gone to see her gentleman friend. She did not seem the least bit surprised nor did she display any concern at all.

It was not very long after I had my visit with that gentleman that information came to me that he was not the only one. Soon after I began teaching at the magnet school, Nicky had started a job at the community college working as a counselor in the students' affairs department. She was there for about eighteen months when she called me at school one day and asked me to meet her at a car dealership. When I met her there, she told me that she had chosen a car for herself and she needed me to cosign for it. I dutifully obliged. It was a brand-new car with monthly payments of over five hundred dollars. We were not making a lot of money, but such was the case with me that whenever she wanted anything, I rarely, if ever, told her no. And so, she drove her spanking-new car off the lot and went home. I followed in my ten-year-old car.

It wasn't a month or two after she purchased her new car that she suddenly announced that she had decided to quit her job. Again, I didn't question her as to her reasons, I just accepted it. But now, the burden of the payments on her car was going to fall squarely on me and the salary I was making as a middle school teacher. It was later on that I learned that she was in fact fired, and part of the reason was because she had started having an affair with one of the staff members in the department.

When I found out about it, I went to see him at the community college. This time, I was not as calm and pleasant as I had been when I met the first guy. I began shouting and making threats to the guy. They had to call security and had me escorted off the campus. A few weeks later, I received a letter saying I was banned completely from the campus and would be arrested if I ever come on the campus again. Apparently, her lover had gone and complained that I had threatened him and he feared for his life, and in an effort to protect him, they banned me from the campus.

Meanwhile, things at home had gone from bad to worse, and it didn't take long for the kids to figure out that the relationship between me and their mother had broken down completely. When they were told some of things that had occurred, none of the first four kids seemed at all surprised. I was shocked that they were not shocked.

"Dad," they said, "we knew this was going on all along, but we were afraid to tell you because you never allowed us to tell you anything negative about Mom."

They were right!

It was soon after that my second son moved out and went to live on his own. From that day until now, he has not been able to bring himself to have anything to do with his mother. Over time, this would become the case with all five kids. While some of the girls will still communicate with her, they do so only with some very specific stipulations.

It Got Worse

THE SITUATION AT home had not gotten any better. It was as if I was living in a trance. I didn't know what to do to get us out of the deep funk in which we found ourselves. And so, we just continued in it. I didn't give any thought to ending the marriage because for some inexplicable reason, I was under the impression that my marriage was something tied to my salvation. So if my marriage failed, then my salvation failed. The other reason was that I knew nothing about the justice system in America and wouldn't know the first step to take to get a divorce. And so, life at home was like being in one miserable rut. I wanted to get out and didn't know how to.

About six months into this situation, I was at school one day when I was called to the office to take a phone call. The person on the line was blunt and to the point.

"Tell your wife," she said, "to leave my husband alone."

I was speechless.

It turned out Nicky was turning up at the first gentleman's workplace still intending to continue her affair with him. His wife had confronted her and told her not to come back there. But according to the wife, Nicky just ignored her and would often turn up to the guy's office even when his wife was there. She and her husband were trying to put their marriage back together, and having the presence of the third party who was part of the reason for their marriage being broken was not helping.

I walked back to my classroom in a daze. I didn't know how I was going to deal with this new situation, and so I called my pastor and asked to come and see him after school. He agreed, and so as soon as I could after school dismissal, I headed to the church. I told the pastor about the phone call I had received earlier in the day, and his reaction was one of painful shock. He called Nicky and asked her to come to the church to meet with him. When she arrived, she didn't seem too surprised to see me there. The pastor then asked her if she hadn't promised to end the affair with the gentleman. With absolutely no sense of concern or shame, her response was "I wasn't going to, but I guess I will have to now."

The pastor and I looked at each other in amazement at the easy and flippant way in which she answered.

I went home that day, knowing that I was not prepared to live like that anymore, and the first thing I did was move out of the marital bedroom. Our son had decided to move out on his own, so his room was not being used and so I decided that would become my room. Sleeping in separate rooms meant that now there was even less interaction between us. I would leave early to go to school before she was up, and most afternoons when I got home, she was not there.

This was a terribly sad time for me because I was concerned how this situation was affecting our kids. The two oldest boys had already moved away from home, one girl was getting ready to go off to college, one was in her junior year of high school, and the other was only five years old. I remembered that my parents had left me when I was barely five years old, and I had vowed that I would never leave my kids. I would always be there for them. I did not know how untenable the situation was going to be in the house, but I was determined that I would stay to ensure that my two youngest girls who were still at home would always have their father with them. But I was soon to find out that what I wanted wasn't necessarily what would happen.

You Have Thirty Minutes to Get Out

APART FROM MY kids, only one other person knew what was going on in my house, and that was my brother who lived in New York. We would often talk on the phone, and he was a major source of encouragement for me. Since my brother and I had gone through so much together, a special bond had developed between us. I was to find out later that Nicky resented the relationship that my brother and I had. I noticed that whenever he would come to visit, she was very cold and distant toward him. And it wasn't that my brother wasn't a terrific guy, he was. He was funny, outgoing, and made friends very easily. The fact that she had a problem with him was only because whenever we were together, it would be some of the happiest and most enjoyable times for me. Whenever he was around, there was always a lot of laughter in the house. The kids loved him too.

And so, it was not surprising that for Christmas of 1996, I asked my brother to come and visit and he agreed. I hadn't told Nicky that he was coming, but she found out anyway. The day my brother arrived was also the final day of school before the Christmas break began. I picked him up at the airport, and we drove home together, laughing and talking like we always do. We were sitting in the living room at home talking when there was a loud knock on the front door. I went to see who or what it was.

When I opened the door, there were two police officers standing there. After asking me my name, one officer sternly said to me, "You have thirty minutes to leave this house."

I was shocked, confused.

"This is my house," I said. "Why would I have to leave?"

What he said next literally left me speechless.

"Your wife has filed a domestic complaint with the court, and you have to leave the residence."

"A domestic complaint?" I asked. "What's that?"

"She says that you have been physically abusing her, and she fears for her life."

"It's not true," I protested.

I could see that from my reaction that the officer had softened toward me somewhat.

"I am sorry," he said, "but there is nothing I can do. You will have to get out of the house, and you have thirty minutes to do so. We'll be waiting outside until you leave."

I closed the door and went back inside.

To say I was shocked and bewildered could not fully express how I felt and what was going through my mind. My brother and I stood there and stared at each other for a long while in total silence. What was most shocking to me was that Nicky had accused me of physical abuse. That was a total lie. If there is one thing that I have always found disgusting, it is a man who beat his wife. I had witnessed my father hit my mother, and I remembered the hatred I felt toward him for doing that. And now to be accused—falsely—of something so horrendous was absolutely astonishing. It is true that I had a temper, but I had never resorted to violence. Not with her or with my kids. It was not something that I would ever want to do to her, no matter the situation. I was always cognizant of the fact that she was the mother of my children, and how could I abuse the woman who had borne my children? Her accusations were total lies.

Still in a daze, I went in my room and began packing some clothing. I had no idea where I was going to go. The police officers were still outside the house waiting for me to leave. As I was packing, I suddenly realized that my brother had just come to visit, and I now had nowhere for him to stay. I asked him to please stay at the house until I could work something out. He refused and said that he would go with me wherever I was going.

I packed my bag, and my brother and I got in my car and drove off, still not knowing where we were going. It was as I was driving that I thought I would drive up to the church and see the pastor. Maybe he could help me. Upon my arrival, I explained to the pastor what had happened. He was sympathetic but said he could not offer any help. He did suggest that maybe I could go to the courts and have the injunction overturned. By this time, it was too late to get to the courthouse to do anything, and so we left the church and just drove around. After a while, it suddenly dawned on me that the only person I knew in Florida was Nicky's brother who lived in Riviera Beach. And so, I decided to drive down there to see if I could stay with him for a while.

He was shocked when I arrived and told him all that had happened, including the parts about his sister's affairs. He was adamant that she would not do such a thing and refused to believe it. He did agree that my brother and I could stay with him, but the only place available for us to sleep was on the floor in the living room. At least it was somewhere to stay while I tried and get my thoughts together.

That Sunday morning, my brother I made our way up from Riviera Beach to attend service at my church. I was a member of the choir and was usually the one who led the nearly one-hundred-member choir up on the platform for praise and worship. I had just taken my place on the platform and was watching as the other members came up when I saw a police officer walk into the sanctuary. He walked up to the platform and indicated for me to follow him. I left the platform and went outside to speak with him.

"You will have to leave," he told me.

Seeing the surprise on my face, he then told me that according to the injunction, I could not be in the same place as my wife, especially if she arrived there before I did. It was then that I saw Nicky standing off to the side with what looked like a cell phone in her hand.

Apparently, she had made it her duty to make sure that she arrived at the church before I did and as soon as I arrived, she called the police to say I was in violation of the injunction. I do not know what it was that I felt at that moment. Was it shame because the whole church had seen me taken off the platform and asked to leave by the police or just disgust that she was so callous that she was prepared to do anything to make my life as miserable as possible? And so, my brother and I got back in my car and drove back down to Riviera Beach.

Now all this had happened the weekend before and so bright and early Monday morning, I was at the courthouse to find out how I could get the injunction overturned so I could return to my house. Finding my way around the court system was totally new to me, and I soon found out that that which I wanted was easier said than done. For one thing, the courts were closed for the holiday, and the earliest I could get to file to overturn the injunction would be in January. I left the courthouse that morning and I wept.

I had always vowed that I would always be there for my children, and here it was Christmas, and I was not even going to get to spend it with them. It was truly one of the saddest days of my life.

The Irony of It

GOING TO STAY with my brother-in-law because I got kicked out of my house was rather ironic for me.

Before he and his family moved to Florida some ten years before, we all lived in the same family house in New York City. His mother had bought the house, and she lived on the top floor, my family lived on the second floor, and my brother-in-law and his family lived on the ground floor. It was not the most ideal situation, but this was New York. Having family around was very helpful especially when I had to be at school at nights and some weekends.

When my mother-in-law purchased the house, she had bought it in my brother-in-law and her names. Despite the fact that he had not contributed anything to the purchase price, he had assumed that the house was also his. At the time, I had four children ranging in age from eleven to five. My two girls were seven and five and it was their practice to sit in the windowsill on the second floor and look out for me when I would come home. They were always the first one to call out to me as I drove up and got out of the car.

One day, I got home, and there they both were at their usual spot calling out to me. As I looked up to respond, I noticed that the mesh that was always in the window was missing. I became very concerned since if the mesh wasn't there and my girls leaned too far out the window, they could easily fall the two stories to the ground.

I immediate inquired as to what had happened with the mesh. They told me that they had pushed on it and it had fallen out, and their uncle had refused to put it back in. I went to find the mesh and the uncle to let him know that I wanted that mesh back in because of my concerns for the safety of my girls. He refused to give me back the mesh, saying that since they had pushed it out of the window, he was not going to put it back in. I told him that my babies' safety was my only concern, and I was going to get the mesh and put it back.

It was then that he attacked me. He swung at me, and I grabbed him around his head and put him in a neck hold. As much as he tried, he could not get loose, so I released him and called him stupid and went to get the mesh. As I turned to go up the stairs to my apartment, he suddenly appeared out of his ground floor apartment with a long butcher knife in his hand and lounged at me with it. He then went back into his apartment and closed the door. I thought he had missed before I noticed that there was some blood on my shirt. I thought nothing of it when I went and called the police because he had attacked me with a knife.

It was while I was seated on the steps outside his apartment waiting for the police to come that I became aware that the flow of blood from my chest was getting worse. I was also getting more and more light-headed as I sat there. The police arrived just at one of those moments. They took one look at me, and I heard one say to the other, "He's not going to make it."

And so, they put me in the squad car and raced me to the hospital, which was about fifteen blocks away. I was put on a gurney, and the last words I remembered hearing were the words "stat, stat" before I lost consciousness.

When I woke up, I was on a respirator, unable to breathe on my own. I was to remain on that respirator for thirteen days before I was taken off. When the doctor came to see me, he told me that they had had to use nearly thirty-two units of blood for my surgery. They had to open my chest to get to the artery that had been nicked, and they also had to pump the blood through my groin to get it into me fast enough. In addition, the doctor said that my lungs had collapsed, and it was a miracle I had survived.

Since I couldn't speak, the nurse had given me a pad to write on for any questions I might have. So I asked the doctor his name. When he told me, I responded, "Oh, you are Jewish?"

"Yes," he said.

"I know another Jewish person too," I wrote.

"Who is that?"

"Jesus," I said.

"Oh," he said, "that was the name you kept repeating while they rolled you into surgery."

When the police officers took me to the hospital, Nicky, who was in the house upstairs, did not make any effort to follow them. It was fortunate for me that my best friend from Jamaica, Headley, had just recently arrived in New York and was staying with us until he could get a place of his own. He arrived at the house almost immediately after the police officers left and quickly followed them to the hospital. When he got to the hospital, they were getting me ready for surgery, and one of the nurses told him that they needed a signature from a family member to proceed with the surgery. He told her he was my brother and signed the consent form and they proceeded with the surgery. Had he not had the presence of mind to go to the hospital, there would have been no one there to sign the consent forms, and who knows what might have been the result. As it was, I was able to have the surgery which was successful, and I was on my way to recovery.

I was in the hospital for two weeks before they sent me home. During that time, I can remember only a few times Nicky came to see me. I didn't think anything of it at the time since I myself was not a fan of hospitals and did not like to visit them since the smell always made me nauseous. I had to spend several more weeks learning to breathe on my own again and worked at getting my physical strength back.

Soon after I got home, I was visited by the police who came to get a statement from me since they had arrested my brother-in-law and were going to charge him with attempted murder. I told them I was not going to press any charges against him. They told me that I would have to come to court and explain that to a judge. Soon afterward, while I was still weak from the surgery, I went to court to explain to the judge that I wanted all the charges against my brother-in-law dismissed. The judge was skeptical as to my reasons for doing so and wanted to find out if I was been paid by someone. I assured him that I was not, and he very reluctantly dismissed the charges and sent my brother-in-law home.

My reason for having the charges against him dismissed actually had nothing to do with him. I was thinking about his wife and their three children, the oldest of whom was only seven years old. I was concerned about the impact it would have on them if he got sent to prison, and I didn't want that for them.

And so, here I was, some twelve years later, reflecting on the irony of having to rely on the man who had almost killed me for a place to stay because his sister had me kicked out of my own house. I was still grateful for small mercies, but after spending a few days with him, I went and rented an apartment of my own.

Unfamiliar Territory

As SOON AS the courthouse opened after the Christmas holiday, I went to file an injunction to have Nicky's injunction against me lifted so I could return to my house. I had informed the kids about what had happened, and each of them decided to write a letter to the judge disputing Nicky's claims of physical abuse.

On the day set for the hearing, the four oldest kids all turned up at court to support me. Nicky was not expecting the boys and our oldest girl to come back to town to offer me their support. As we waited outside the courtroom for the hearing, Nicky approached me and said she wanted to speak to me. I told her that anything she had to say to me, she could say in front of the kids. I was not going to put myself in any situation that she could use to say I did her harm. And so, with the four kids listening, she told us that she had cancer and was going to need to have surgery. Shock upon shock! All of a sudden, any sense of bitterness or anger toward her dissipated, and I became very concerned. We all began to ask her questions that she refused to answer.

It was while this was going on that a police officer came out and told us that the judge was ready for us. When I walked in, still in shock from what Nicky had just told us, I didn't know what to expect. The judge spoke and said Nicky had withdrawn her injunction against me, and there was no need to proceed any further. Suddenly, I was very angry again.

"Your Honor," I said, "she has made some scandalous statements against me that were now part of the public record that I need to refute."

"I am sorry," he said, "since she has withdrawn her injunction, there is nothing else I can do."

"This is ridiculous," I shouted.

It was then that the police officer, who was the bailiff I assumed, said to me, "You cannot speak to the judge like that."

"You shut up!" was my retort.

I continued to protest to the judge and I could see that while he had some sympathy for my position, he was insistent that there was nothing he could do.

While all this was going on, Nicky just stood there and said nothing. As we walked out of the courtroom, she came over to me and put her hand in mine, and a sense of concern for her suddenly flooded my whole being again.

We all drove back to the house, and I was still in the dark as to the situation with her health. As we drove back to the house, I began to make arrangements for my son to take over the apartment that I had recently rented since I was now going to have to return home in light of her medical situation. But as much as we asked, she was not forthcoming with any details. It was then that my daughter called me aside and said, "Dad, what if she is lying?"

I hadn't thought of that. But now, I was beginning to give it some thought. She had gone and filed for that injunction against me based on lies and then had suddenly decided to drop it without an explanation to anyone.

When we arrived at the house, I was still in a state of uncertainty. Soon after we arrived at the house, phone rang. Since I was standing closest to it, I moved to answer it.

"Don't answer it," Nicky said.

I couldn't understand why not, so I took up the phone and said hello. It was her sister calling from New York to check on her. I took the opportunity to ask the sister how they could have allowed her to have done to me what she did when they knew it wasn't true. Her response was that her sister had told her that I had abused her and she believed it. Despite my protestation, she was not about to change her mind. I hung up the phone, and Nicky, who was standing there staring at me, said, "I told you not to answer it." She then walked off.

It was then and there that I decided that enough was enough and that I was going to leave the house to her and go back to my apartment. I realized that my anger at her lies were still very much with me, and I couldn't see myself coming back home and pretending as if nothing had happened. When I told her that I was in fact not coming back to the house, she pleaded with me to stay. Despite her pleading, I was somehow able to muster up what little courage I had and walked out the door. It was not an easy thing to do.

Back into Court

IF I THOUGHT that Nicky was going to use the fact that I had moved out of the house as an opportunity for her to do some self-assessments and change her behavior in order to get me to move back home, I was sadly mistaken. It wasn't too long after that I was served with another notice to appear in court.

Like I said, at the time, I knew very little about how the American judicial system worked. And so, I turned up to court all by myself. She came with a lawyer. I found out that he was a high-priced lawyer from a nearby county. I had no idea how she came to be his client. Before the judge, the lawyer began to accuse me of having abandoned my family. He said that Nicky was the only one taking care of the two girls who were still at home and that I was not providing any financial support to them. I explained to the judge that I had my own apartment but was still paying the mortgage on the house and that she had refused to go out and try and find a job. Her lawyer then told the judge that the only thing Nicky really wanted was for me to return home. And so, the judge ordered that we should go to mediation.

We must have gone to at least three mediations sessions ordered by the court, and nothing changed. When she saw that I was not ready to return home simply because that was what she wanted, she would have me served again and again with notices to appear in court. I was getting fed up with it and wondered how they could be allowing her to keep doing that. I would come to find out that the court system doesn't usually try and determine what had been done before. They were only dealing with what was happening now. Eventually, we were brought before a judge who demanded that she should go and get a psychological examination done. I never did find out what the results of that examination showed or if she even went and had one done.

I had to have a new phone put in the apartment I rented and only gave my girls the number so they could call when they wanted to. It didn't take long for Nicky to somehow get the number and start making what I could only call harassing phone calls. She would call me several times each day, demanding that I come home. Sometimes, she would make promises about trying to make things better between us, but other times, she was belligerent and angry. I never returned any of her calls.

It was about four months after I moved out of the house that I decided to go and see a lawyer about the possibility of a divorce. Divorce was still not something that I really wanted. After speaking with the lawyer a number of times, I still could not bring myself to begin the proceedings to get a divorce. I could see that the lawyer was getting frustrated with my reluctance to move ahead with the divorce. She told me to either make up my mind or find another lawyer since I was wasting her time. I told her to go ahead and file.

Attacked

THE LAWYER HAD told me that after the divorce papers were filed, a copy would be sent to Nicky by mail. I had decided to get on with my life and had decided that things were now over between us.

I was in my classroom about a week after filing the divorce papers when the door to my classroom was suddenly burst open, and in walked Nicky who began attacking me in front of my students. Shocked, I tried to hold her off while she used her hands and then her shoes to try and hit me in the face and on my head. When that didn't work, she then picked up a big rock I used to keep my classroom door open and started hitting me with it. My students sat there in stunned silence, watching what was happening.

Apparently, she had just that day received a copy of the divorce papers, and she got so angry that she drove the twenty miles from her house to the school to attack me. She was going on and on about something as she was hitting me, but I wasn't able to determine what it was she was saying as I was too busy defending myself against her angry barrage. A teacher next door, hearing the commotion, called the school office and asked for the resource officer to come. He came to find her still trying to assault me and me trying to defend myself. She was arrested and taken away. I was very shaken up and, once again, found myself in total shock at being humiliated again by her in front of other people.

The deputy sheriff, whom we both knew, would bail her out of jail after she was charged with domestic violence. The irony of that was not lost on me. Here was a woman who had falsely claimed that I had physically abused her, and here she had been arrested for that very thing against me. When she was asked why she had attacked me, her response was that she did not attack me, she had just come to the school to pray for me.

After the commotion was over, the principal called me and told me to go home and take a few days off. I did.

That particular incident was to make me the butt of the jokes on morning talk radio. The hosts had a field day talking about a husband who got his butt whipped in front of his students at his school. I didn't think there was anything funny about it, but apparently, it was good fodder for morning radio for a few days.

After about three days, I returned to school and to my classroom to find my desk stacked with cards from many of my students. All of them expressed sympathy for what had happened to me. There were some that I found particularly satisfying. Some students expressed their appreciation for me living what I taught. I had often mentioned to them how abhorrent it was for any man to hit a female, and they said they were glad to see me practice that when I didn't hit back when she attacked me.

After she was released from jail, she would call the morning radio program, sending good wishes to me and expressing her undying love as well. I never heard any of her calls. It was other people who told me that she was doing it.

That attack against me in front of my students was not her only attempt to humiliate me. Oftentimes, when we went to church, there was a young lady there who I would often have conversation with. Her hands were always cold, and for some reason, mine were always warm. And so, she would stick her hands into mine to warm them up. That was all there was to it. We had never had any conversation with each other away from the church. We had never been to each other's house, and we didn't even know each other's phone number, much less to have had any conversation on the phone. Nicky knew this, but in an effort to find something with which to besmirch me, she went to the pastor of the church to tell him that I was having an affair with this lady. Of course, the pastor called her in, and she had to assure him that those allegations were not true. The pastor didn't bother to call me in as I supposed that since he knew Nicky's history of having affairs, he knew that she was probably trying to paint me in as bad a light as possible.

Nicky's crusade against me didn't stop there. When she found out that I had also spoken to another lady at the church, she went to the lady's employment place and asked for her boss to tell her that she was the one responsible for the breakup of our marriage. The lady's boss refused to entertain her nonsense and told her that if she didn't get off the property, she would have her arrested.

The amazing thing was during all that was going on, not once did she apologize for anything she had done. She just kept playing the victim, and a victim she was not.

Between having me dragged into court time after time and going around spreading false allegations against me, Nicky was making it easier for me to go through with the divorce, but I still hesitated.

Finally, the lawyer called me in one day and told me that I had to pay her the total amount she would be paid if I had gone through with the divorce. In addition, she was dropping me as a client and I should find someone else. She handed me all my papers in an envelope, and I walked out of her office still very much uncertain about getting a divorce.

Attacked Again

IT WAS APPROACHING the time for the lease on my apartment to be renewed when Nicky sent word to me that she was thinking of moving way and going to live in Canada. She planned to take our youngest child with her, and she wanted to know if I had any money to give her that she could use to help tide them over until she got herself properly settled. Now despite all the things she had done to me and all the lies she had told, I kept remembering that she was still the mother of my children. And so, I gave her all the money I had at the time, about eleven hundred dollars, and she purportedly left for Canada to go and live with a girlfriend of hers.

Since the lease on my apartment was up and the house was going to be empty, I decided to go back to the house and live there with the only daughter who was now still at home.

About two weeks after I moved in, my other daughter was home visiting from college. We were there just sitting around talking when we heard a knock at the door. I opened the door, and there standing in the doorway was Nicky and my baby girl. She barged right past me into the house with her briefcase and announced that she was coming back home since she didn't like it in Canada. She went into the bedroom and came out dressed in her pajamas.

Once again, I couldn't help but be shocked at her behavior. I immediately went into the closet and began packing my stuff to leave. As I was in the closet, she came and stood in the door, imploring me not to leave. I told her that there was no way I was going to stay in the same house with her and continued packing. It was then she walked into the closet and began attacking me again. She tore the glasses from my face and was attempting to hit me in my face when our oldest daughter came in and dragged her off me.

That same daughter was the one who called the police, and when they came, she was arrested again for domestic violence against me. They took her away still dressed in her pajamas. I unpacked my stuff and stayed because now, I had two of my girls with me in the house.

We were in the house for about another two weeks when I again heard knocking at the door. When I went to check, there were two police officers standing there. They told me that I had to leave the house again. Apparently, during the course of one of her rampages against me, she had gone to court again and gotten an order allowing her to stay in the house. After she was arrested, her mother had bailed her out and took her to live at her house. While she was there, she remembered the court order she had gotten and decided that she was going to have it enforced by having me put out of the house again. And so, in the space for six months, I again found myself homeless.

I immediately went back to the apartment complex where I had rented my last apartment to find out if they had any available. They had an apartment that just recently come available, and so I was fortunate to have been homeless for only a few hours that day.

When the time came for the domestic violent charges against her to be heard in court, I told the court that I did not wish to pursue those charges against her. I was told that the only way they could be dropped was if I attended meetings at a safe space for battered spouses. And so, in order to not let the mother of my children end up in jail, I started going to meetings for abused spouses. I was the only male at those meetings, and after attending all the required sessions, they dropped the charges against her.

I Don't Care

DESPITE ALL THAT had happened, I still had not gone through with the divorce. Everything was in limbo until I got another notice to appear in court. All the other times, I had gone on my own, but this time, I decided to get a lawyer to go with me. She and her high-priced lawyer were probably not expecting that when I turned up for court. I told the judge that I was going to go through with the divorce, and he ordered a mediation to determine the division of assets.

The date was set for us and our lawyers to meet. When the meeting began, my wife suddenly got up and said, "He can have it all, I don't care."

My lawyer quickly wrote down what she said, had her sign it, and she walked out.

It was obvious that in a moment of frustration, she had decided to make that statement, and my lawyer wasn't going to give her a chance to change her mind. My lawyer drafted an agreement giving me custody of the two girls, who were still minors, possession of the house and all real property, and for her to start paying me child support after two years. When the agreement was signed, the judge granted me a divorce at 1:15 p.m. on January 28, 1998. I walked out of that courthouse a free man, went and got my two girls, and we went home.

By the time of the divorce, the children had watched as their mother told one lie after another and did several despicable things to me, and they too had had enough of her. All of them refused to have anything whatsoever to do with her after the divorce.

After she had me kicked out of the house the last time, she had gone to the courts several times to file injunctions against several of the kids, including the one still living at the house with her. She claimed that she was in danger of her life from them and wanted the court to order them out of the house. She did not wait for the court to respond before she packed up our daughter's clothing, put them in two black garbage bags, and put her out of the house. Someone saw her walking down the street carrying the bags of clothing and offered to take her in.

It wasn't long after the divorce that I was to hear from my ex-wife. This time, she was lamenting the fact that none of the children wanted to have anything to do with her. She said she was planning to move to New York to live with her sister and wondered if I would let our youngest daughter, who was only seven years old at the time, come and live with her. I was torn. I really felt sorry for her, and it was true that only the seven-year-old seemed to have any positive regard toward her. I reluctantly agreed after having her sign a note stating that she knew that I was the one who had full custody of our daughter and I could come and get her anytime.

I was to live to regret ever agreeing to let her take my daughter with her to New York.

The Kiss

It was one of those things that you didn't plan for and certainly wasn't expecting, but yet it happened. Such was the case with me and Mary.

It was a particularly difficult time in my life. In the middle of studying for a doctoral degree, I was confronted with a cheating wife who had made it clear that she no longer had any interest in working on our marriage of nearly twenty-five years. It was becoming more and more obvious that she had chosen to go her own way, and I was no longer going to be part of her life. I was devastated. I thought my whole life was about to end. I contemplated a miserable future to come. The one thing I did not want to become was a statistic. And yet, I was about to become one. A divorced person, I had known no one in my family who had gone through a divorce. I was the first.

I was confused, miserable, and angry, but I had work to do. There were doctoral assignments that had to be done. They were the only things that kept me going. While I concentrated on getting my work done, I had very little time to think about the misery of my situation.

I was not aware at first of the effect the divorce had on me until it began to impact the students in my classroom. I had always been a teacher who tried to maintain a very positive atmosphere in the classroom. With the divorce, that began to change, and I was getting more and more angry with the kids.

One day, the students in one of my classes were being particularly noisy, and I exploded in anger, and I kicked over the garbage can in the classroom, leaving a huge dent in it. At the same time, I shouted at the kids, "Shut the hell up." There was a stunned silence around the room.

The following day, I was called into the principal's office and reprimanded for my unprofessional behavior. Some of the kids even told their parents that they feared for their safety after I exploded in anger.

And so, it was one Sunday morning, as I stood with my back against the wall waiting to go up on the platform, I was miserable. Over twenty-five years of my life was disintegrating before my eyes. It was about that time for the choir to go up on the platform. The church service was about to begin. I was deep in thought when suddenly, there was a voice beside me.

"What's the matter with you?"

I turned and looked. Her name was Mary, and while we had seen each other before and said hello, she had never paid any particular attention to me, so I was a bit taken aback by her question.

"What's the matter with you?" she asked again.

"Oh," I blurted out. "My marriage is over. My wife has been having numerous affairs, and I have gotten tired of it."

I could see the look of shock on her face as she quickly walked away as if to say, "I don't want any part of that."

Mary was one of the most likable persons I had ever met. She had a ready smile for everyone and had a very friendly personality. I had never seen her be anything but upbeat and smiling. People were easily drawn to her. I liked her, but I knew that she didn't particularly like me.

One Sunday morning, as we were getting ready to go up on the platform to start praise and worship, the ladies in the choir were just chatting away, and I got very annoyed with it.

"Will you all please shut up," I shouted at them.

Mary was standing nearby and turned and looked at me in amazement at my outburst.

That was not my only negative encounter with her. After practice one night, I asked her if she could give me a drive home since I didn't have my car and I lived not too far from her. She agreed, and when I got in her car, I began to use my feet to move her cassette tapes that she had on the car floor. I could tell from the look on her face that she was not pleased. I think she immediately regretted agreeing to give me that drive home.

Another time I was having problems with my mortgage and since she worked in mortgage, I had asked her for help with the problems I was having. When she arrived at the house, I was on the phone berating the person on the other end of the phone line. When I handed her the phone, I could hear her saying things like "Yes," "You're right," "You would think so." I could tell, and she would later confirm that the person on the phone was telling her what a jerk I was and she was readily agreeing.

As painful as it was that Sunday morning, I was able to get through the church service. As I was coming off the platform, I felt a touch on my arm. I turned around. It was Mary.

"Here," she said. "Here is my phone number, call me if you ever need someone to talk to."

"Thanks," I said, surprised at her offer as I put the piece of paper in my pocket.

It was a Sunday afternoon, and I had gone to church as usual and was back home sitting at my desk trying to bury my sorrows in my work when the phone rang.

"Hello."

"Hi."

It was Mary. I was very surprised to receive a call from her.

"I am going to my office to do some work," she said. "If you want to, you can come by, and we can talk."

"Sure," I said. "I would love to come."

It was not that I particularly wanted to talk to anyone. It was just nice to be asked.

It was about five o'clock when I pulled my car into the parking lot at Mary's office. I noticed her car was parked nearby. As I got out of the car and walked toward her office door, I was thinking how nice it was to get away from the books for a change. I needed something else to do to ease my mind other than the constant studying. I knocked on her office door. It was locked. I knocked again. Suddenly, there she was.

She opened the door with a friendly "Hi," and I responded in kind. I was nervous. I don't know why, but I was nervous. I followed her into her office, and for the next hour or so, I sat there and poured out my hurt, pain, and anger to a person who, though I knew her, was still very much a stranger to me. She listened. I could tell that she really felt for me. It was as if she knew my pain. *What an extraordinarily understanding person*, I thought. I was to learn later on that her understanding demeanor was because she herself had experienced similar pains as mine.

It was getting late and time for me to get back home to my girls, back to my books, back to the loneliness and the misery of my situation. I got up to leave and followed her to the door. Suddenly she stopped, turned, and looked at me. *What now?* I thought. There was a questioning look in her eyes. It was as if there was something she wanted to ask me, but didn't quite know how to go about asking. Being shorter than me, she looked up at me and asked the one question I was not expecting.

"Would you mind if I kissed you?" My heart skipped a beat. My mouth dropped open. Sweat suddenly appeared on my brow. I had no response at first. I guess I was in shock. It was not the kind of question I was expecting, especially from a lady whom I knew was not particularly fond of my angry outbursts that she was familiar with.

"I thought you would never ask," I stammered.

I walked up to her. She was such a little thing, so petite. We embraced, and as I looked down into her eyes, I could see that there was caring and genuine concern there. Her lips parted. My lips parted. Our lips met. Time stopped. My heart stopped. My whole world stopped. My body shook. Was that electricity passing through me? I felt nothing. I was numb.

After what seemed like an eternity, very, very slowly, I let go of her. I was breathing deeply. Breath was coming to my lungs in rapid gasps. I looked at her. She looked at me. Not a word was said, but we knew. That kiss had changed everything forever. We were never going to be the same again.

A New Beginning

IT WAS ABOUT six months after my divorce that I married Mary. Now to some people, that might seem like that was too fast. It wasn't for me. For one thing, I had no interest in living a single lifestyle. I was surprised to find out how many women suddenly became interested in me as a single man. One incident in particular stood out.

I was in my apartment one afternoon when I heard a knock on my door. When I opened the door, it was one of my students. His mother had sent him to ask me if I liked banana nut bread. I told him I did. He asked if I minded if he used my phone to call and let his mother know. No problem, I said. What I would later find out was that was what his mother had told him to do so my phone number could come up on her caller ID. From that day on, I would get several phone calls from the mother inviting to meet her at various places. Mind you, this was a married woman living at home with her husband. I told her I was not interested, but that didn't stop her phone calls. Finally, I got fed up and told her in no uncertain terms that she was not my type and I had no interest in her. I was appalled, and having just come out of a relationship where I was the victim of an unfaithful wife made it all the more galling to me. But I was a family man with a strong belief in the institution of marriage, and that was that.

There was also another reason why we got married as quickly as we did. One afternoon, I was driving home and I had an open vision. I called it an open vision because I was wide awake and saw this unfold before me. I had never had anything like that happen to me before and, in fact, had always been skeptical of people who claimed to have visions.

In the vision, I saw Mary (or Scottie as I had now began calling her) talking to one of her best friend and was sharing with her that we were planning to get married. That was all I saw. When I got home, I called Scottie and told her what had happened. She started to laugh. I didn't think anything I had shared was funny. After she stopped laughing, she said, "You are not going to believe this."

She then went on to relate that she had met that very day with her friend that I had seen in the vision and had told her about us for the first time. To her surprise, her friend smiled at her and said, "I knew it all along. The Lord had told me you two would be married, and I had written it down in my journal several months ago."

I was thunderstruck.

Like I said, I had always been a skeptic when it came to such things, but now that it had actually happened to me, I became a believer.

Scottie had also told me that the Lord had revealed to her that we would be married, but she didn't believe it since after seeing my display of temper, she was certain that I wasn't the man for her. But now, here we both were, making a commitment to forge a relationship based on love, commitment, and trust when all we had experienced in our lives so far was anything but those things. But somehow, I knew that it was a challenge we could both meet and are meeting together. And so, in June of 1998, I got married again. This time, I was not that young, inexperienced twenty-year-old but a mature, educated man in his midforties.

The wedding was a very simple affair with just family members and a few very close friends. It took place at nine o'clock in the morning. We planned it that way because that afternoon, I had to be in Fort Lauderdale for my graduation for my doctoral degree. All my kids were there to give their blessings, and the two boys told me that they were going to be particularly on the alert in case their mother turned up and try to disrupt the wedding. It was something that she was quite capable of doing, and they wanted to make sure it didn't happen. The fact that she was somewhere up in New York might be the reason she wasn't able to try and disrupt what was otherwise a very pleasant occasion on a day that was bright and sunny.

One of Scottie's best friends paid for the entire wedding reception. So all we had to do was turn up, and when the time was right, we left for my graduation and then for a Caribbean cruise.

We had just gotten back from our honeymoon cruise and had just walked through the door when the house phone rang. We had decided to move into my Scottie's house instead of staying in mine. She answered the phone, and at the end of the line was my ex-wife calling to congratulate her on her wedding to me. She proceeded to making some disparaging remarks about me before Scottie, in no uncertain terms, made it clear to her that she was not interested in any of her comments and she should never call our house gain.

That phone call I believe was what led to a five-year battle for me to have contact with my youngest daughter whom I had agreed could move with her mother to New York. That was one very big mistake on my part.

They Need Someone Like You

BEFORE THE BREAKUP of my marriage, I had gone on several mission trips to Jamaica during the summer months. I had always gone alone since my former wife had to stay home with the kids. I know that she probably could not go, but the thing that I never understood was her total lack of interest in any of the work I did while on these trips. I don't recall her ever asking me how things went. It was just one of those weird things that I couldn't quite figure out at the time.

Now that I had recently remarried, I was asked again to resume going on these annual trips to Jamaica. About five years had passed since I had been on the last one. It was after I had returned from my last trip, only to find out that my marriage was crumbling. I had vowed then not to go on any more of those trips until I resolved the problems within the marriage. Well, after several years trying to make it work and finally coming to the conclusion that the wife had no such interest, I had finally gotten a divorce.

Unlike my ex-wife, Scottie was very interested in going on these mission trips with me, and I readily agreed. It was while we were one such trip that I began to give some thoughts to returning to Jamaica to work.

We had spent about four days doing daily Bible classes and other activities in a part of the poorer section of the town when the coordinator of the trip, Desi, decided that everyone needed a day off. Early the next morning, we all piled into the vehicles and made our way to the beach in Negril. Negril is one of the truly beautiful areas in Jamaica that is visited by thousands of tourists each year. Since Scottie and I were not too interested in getting in the water, we just sat at a table on the beach talking. We were joined by Desi, and we decided to order some lunch from the restaurant nearby. Since Desi was the only one who knew exactly what he wanted, the waitress took his order and soon returned with his meal. She said she would be back to take our order. Desi ate his meal and left, and still, the waitress hadn't returned to take our order. So we decided that we would walk further down the beach to find another restaurant.

We had just taken our seats facing the water at new restaurant when I saw what looked like a familiar figure walking toward us. I was not certain at first, but soon I realized that it was Esther, the only girl in the Mead family. We greeted each and began chatting to catch up with what had been happening with each other. It had been a few years since I had last seen her, and she could obviously see that I now had a new bride. As we talked, she told me that she had decided to return to Jamaica to live and teach. Esther was one of the three children who was born in Jamaica, and so she had dual citizenship. After her marriage ended in divorce, she wanted to get as far away from England as possible, and so she came back to Jamaica and was teaching at a boarding high school for boys located in a nearby parish.

Esther then began to tell me about the school's inability to find the right person for the position of principal (or headmaster). She suggested that since I was teaching in the States and was well qualified for the position, I should apply. Now I had not given much thought before then of returning to work or live in Jamaica, and while the idea intrigued me, I was not sold on it.

"They need someone like you," she said.

"All right," I said, "I will give it some thought."

She took my number and promised that she would contact the chairman of the school board to let him know to expect my application.

I returned to the States and promptly forgot everything about the job in Jamaica. It was in late September when I got a call from Esther, and she wanted to know if I had followed up with an application for the job. I told her that I had not. She said that the chairman had been expecting to hear from me, and when he hadn't, he had called her to follow up with me. Although I was still not certain that was what I wanted to do, I sent in the application for the position.

Nearly two months went by and I had heard nothing. Once again, I put it out of my mind. Then just as we were getting ready for the Thanksgiving break from school, I got a call from the chairman inviting me to come to Jamaica for an interview. I was still uncertain, and besides, I did not have the funds to purchase a ticket to fly to Jamaica for only a two-day stay. I was strongly inclined to tell him that I would not be coming.

I was still trying to make up my mind when a friend of ours called and said he understood that I was thinking of not going to Jamaica for the interview. His wife was Scottie's best friend, and she had mentioned to her about my reluctance.

"You have to go," he said, "and I will give you the money for the plane ticket."

And that was how I found myself on a plane to Jamaica the day before Thanksgiving. I was going to be interviewed for a job that I was not all that certain I really wanted.

The Interview

When I arrived in Jamaica, I was met at the airport by several members of the school board. Apparently, they were very enthusiastic about the possibility of me coming and wanted me to know it.

They had made all the arrangements for my stay at no expense to me, and after I was dropped off at the hotel where I was staying, I was informed that the interview would take place the following day and that there would be at least six people taking part, including someone from the Ministry of Education. I was a little nervous but not particularly worried since I was not too concern about whether I was offered the job or not. I had only come because my friend had paid for the flight. And so, after having some dinner, I went to my room, took a shower, and went to sleep.

The interview was going to be held in one of the hotel's conference room starting at ten o'clock. I was up early, had some breakfast, put on a suit, and went down to the lobby to wait about fifteen minutes before the scheduled time. I have always had a strong aversion to being late for anything. It makes me nervous, and I didn't want to appear nervous that morning.

The interview started promptly at ten, and like I was told, there were about six people doing the interview. There was one person representing the Ministry of Education, one representing the Munro Dickenson Trust, and the others I assumed were members of the school board. After introduction all around, the questioning began. I really wasn't nervous about answering any of the questions asked as

I was not trying to go out of my way to impress anyone. I answered each question as calmly and as frankly as I could.

As the questioning proceeded, I began to become aware that there was one particular gentleman who was giving the impression that he was not impressed with me at all. It didn't matter to me, and maybe that was the reason for what happened next.

"Dr. Hendricks," he said, speaking with an air of condescension as he addressed me, "do you believe in the theory of evolution?"

Now the gentleman would have known from my application that I had just recently being ordained a minister of the gospel. So I assumed that either he was trying to be provocative or he thought that he was going to catch me with a gotcha question.

"No, I don't," I replied calmly.

"How can you call yourself an educated man with a doctoral degree and not believe in evolution?" His voice was dripping with sarcasm.

"Sir," I responded, "it's interesting isn't it that after more than a hundred years after Darwin first put forward his theory that it is still being called the theory of evolution. One would have thought that had it proven to be valid that they would have dropped the 'theory' part, but the fact that they haven't should be a clear indicator that it is still only a theory."

He looked at me, I looked at him, and he said nothing else. Someone at the table though did make a funny comment about it right at the moment that I took a mouthful of orange juice from my glass. In an attempt to stop myself from laughing, I spewed the orange juice all over the gentleman who had set himself up to be my antagonist during the interview. He didn't ask me another question after that.

The interview lasted from ten o'clock until about one when the chairman asked me to step outside the room while they consulted. I walked out and went and sat in the lobby and waited. About half an hour later, the representative from the Minister of Education came down the stairs, shook my hand, and said she had to leave. Another half an hour passed before I was summoned back to the conference room.

The chairman spoke.

"After our discussion," he said, "we have decided to offer you the position of headmaster at Munro College started next September."

I was numb. I must have said thank you or something to that effect because soon after that, they left the conference room, and I went back to my room and hyperventilated. I had no idea what I was getting myself into, and after spending the rest of the day just lying in bed, I got up early the following morning to catch my flight back home.

Munro College

WHEN I WAS going to high school, Munro College was one of, if not the most prestigious high school for boys in the entire country. It was where the wealthy people sent their boys to school. Ambassadors and other foreign dignitaries who were assigned to work in Jamaica also made it their first school of choice.

Munro was known for its outstanding academic achievements and can boast at least one prime minister and several ministers of government among its alumni or "old boys" as they were called. And it was not just in academics that Munro excelled. It was a power-house school, too, for athletic achievements as well. It truly was the elite high school for boys in the island.

The school was also unique in that it was a boarding school located way out in the country far away from what would be considered civilization. It meant that most of the boys lived on the campus and were only allowed to leave and go home for visits once a month. Discipline at the school was very strict, and caning (or paddling) was allowed as a form of discipline.

I was born in a little village called Round Hill just down the hill from where the school is located, perched on a hill about three thousand feet above sea level. It was not by coincidence that the motto of the school is "A city set on a hill cannot be hid." People from my little village were not even allowed to go on the campus unless they were day workers who did the cleaning and the cooking for the boys and the staff.

While thousands of boys have gone through the school in the over one hundred and fifty years of its existence, by the time I was appointed, I was only the thirteenth headmaster in the history of the school. I was also the first one that could be considered black. All the previous headmasters before me had all being white men. The last one had resigned some three years before, and the school had been unable to find a suitable person to replace him, and so for the four years before I got there, they had someone serving an acting headmaster.

Apparently, the school had fallen on hard times in those recent years and was no longer regarded to be as prestigious as it once was. I was told by the chairman that one of my primary responsibilities was to restore the school to its former position of academic excellence. I would have nearly a full year to think about what I had agreed to and to determine how and what I intended to do to achieve the chairman's directive.

Baka Yaard (Back Home to Jamaica)

By the beginning of the summer, I had shipped most of my furniture and other things to Jamaica. My wife and I were also helping out with the annual mission trip that our friend Desi had been arranging for several years. We arrived in Jamaica some three months before I was to start my new job at Munro.

Now my wife had been on a few mission trips to Jamaica with me before, and there had been no problem whatsoever. However, on this trip, she suddenly was having cold feet about moving to Jamaica. She was born in Florida and lived there all her life. Going on mission trips was one thing since she knew that within a week, she would be back home to familiar territory. Now however, the thought of having to live in Jamaica permanently began to present a major challenge for her. One of her main concerns was the problem she was having understanding what people were saying. People in the country spoke a form of the Jamaican dialect that was impossible for her to understand. So I had to be her translator. That was a situation that she was willing to accept for a week or so but not on a permanently basis.

The night before we were to move up to Munro and the day before the other Americans on the mission trip were to head back to the States was a really trying one for me. My wife was very upset and crying, saying that she wanted to go home. I was trying my best to persuade her to stay with me and for us to face this new adventure together. She was having none of it. We must have been going back and forth with our discussion for about three hours before she finally calmed down and agreed to stay. It was not to be the last time that I would have had to beg, plead, and cajole her to stay in Jamaica and don't leave to go back to the States.

It was in November of 2000 that I was offered the job of headmaster of Munro College, and it would be September 2001 before I would take up my position. For that entire year that I spent teaching in Florida, I had no idea about the specific conditions that existed at Munro. During the Easter break of 2001, I was invited to come to Jamaica to be introduced to the students as their new headmaster. When I arrived on the campus, I was shock at what I saw. The place didn't look anything like how I remembered it when I visited as a schoolboy. The then-headmaster was a personal friend of Mr. Mead and would often invite him to come and speak at Christian events. I would often accompany Mr. Mead on some of those trips and was often intrigued at this place that was once off limits to me. It was like walking on hallowed grounds to me back then.

Now here I was visiting for the first time in over thirty years, and it looked nothing like I remembered. That certain allure that the place had back then was missing, and many of the buildings looked old and run-down. After spending a day on campus meeting some of the students and members of the staff, I left wondering what I had gotten myself into when I agreed to accept the job.

During the year I was waiting to come to Munro, I was only able to get snippets of information about the school and its operations. There was no comprehensive set of information that I could have that would help me make specific plans for the school. I realized that if I was going to get a handle on things, I would have to arrive on the campus months before I was officially supposed to take up the position. And so it was that I arrived in Jamaica in June even though I wasn't slated to officially start working until September.

Once I arrived on campus, I set about meeting the people who were in charge, including the acting headmaster, and began to familiarize myself with everything regarding the school. One of the first things I asked to see was the time table, the daily schedule of classes for the boys. I was shocked when I saw that each class lasted for only thirty minutes. Thirty minutes! How much could any teacher get anything done in thirty minutes? As I thought about it, I was thinking that it would probably take the boys about ten minutes to move from one class to the other. Then it would probably take the teacher another five to ten minutes to take the roll and get the class settled to begin teaching. That would leave just about ten minutes for doing any viable teaching at all! It was ridiculous.

Much to the chagrin of those responsible for making up the time table, I demanded that there had to be changes made before the school year began. I wanted classes to be for at least one hour. The core classes like English, math, and the sciences were to be taught every day, and the other classes were to be scheduled based on their order of importance. It meant that a class like agricultural science would only need to be scheduled for once per week. Physical education was to be taught at least three times each week for the lower classes and only once a week, if at all, for the boys in the upper school. As much as they weren't happy to have to do the entire time table over again, it was done and ready to go by the time the boys arrived on campus for the first day of school.

Trouble upon Trouble

THERE WERE A number of incidents that occurred within a month of my being at Munro that were to define my entire time there.

The first occurred just a day after school began. A teacher brought a boy to me to complain that he was calling her derogatory names. Now students calling teachers names was just the norm among high schools in Jamaica. Any indication that the name bothered the teacher meant that they would continue to be called that name for as long as possible. Students could be merciless in using the name particularly if it was an offensive one. They would quickly stop, however, if it appears that the teacher was not in the least bit bothered by it. The thing was though that some of the names were so memorable that they were very hard to ignore.

A student had to be careful not to get caught when calling the teacher that name. Apparently, this boy was not smart enough, and so here he was standing before me and insisting that the teacher was lying. I was inclined to believe the teacher because of what he said when I asked him if he had called her the name she mentioned.

"She's lying," he said.

It was interesting to me that he didn't say that he hadn't done that; instead, he called her a liar to her face and in front of me. I told him I believed the teacher and insisted that he apologize or I would cane (paddle) him. He reluctantly did so, and they left my office.

It was after they left my office that it occurred to me that the teacher was the wife of the gentleman who upon till a few days earlier was the acting headmaster. So why didn't she take the boy to him since he would have been more familiar with the boy and would know if that kind of behavior was what he was capable of? I was to learn later that I was probably been set up.

The second incident occurred at the beginning of my second week and was directly related to the first incident. I was in my office when my secretary knocked and came in to tell me that Mrs. Neil and her husband were outside and wanting to see me. Ah, Mrs. Neil!

Mrs. Neil was the assistant principal. She had been away on leave, supposedly working on her master's degree. Even though she had been invited to the various functions that had been held to introduce me to the school and the surrounding community, she had never once turned up for any of them. I knew her before I came to Munro. She was a fellow student at the teachers' college I attended. At the time, she was unmarried and her maiden name was Powell. While in college, she was not the kind of person that I would have had any contact with and I didn't. I had not seen or heard from her since our graduation in June of 1973. So why she would be coming to see me now? I had absolutely no idea, but I was intrigued.

"Send her in," I said.

Mrs. Neil and her husband bounded into my office, and I could tell from the looks on their faces that this was not a social call. She immediately addressed me.

"Good morning, Dr. Hendricks." And she said it with the flourish of someone trying to speak like an English aristocracy.

"Morning, Mrs. Neil. How can I help you?"

She then launched into a tirade about me wanting to cane her son for no reason at all and she wanted to know why. Before I could even respond, her husband started boisterously declaring that if I had lain a hand on his son, what he would have done to me. I looked at him. He was a very short man who reminded me of the typical ignorant Jamaican male, full of talk and bluster and nothing else. I had no idea what they were talking about. It was then she told me about the incident where the teacher had brought a boy to me for calling her a derogatory name. The boy was her son. I hadn't made the connection.

What was interesting to me was her son had not been caned. I had only threatened to do so if he failed to apologize to the teacher. But now, having not made any attempt to contact me in the past, here she was thinking that it was important that she came to see me to challenge my authority. As soon as her husband began making threats, I asked them to step outside my office while I made a telephone call to the chairman of the school board. They left the office and stood outside the opened door listening while I was on the phone. As I was relaying to the chairman what had happened, Mr. Neil could clearly be heard at the door shouting, "He's lying, 'di bwoy' a tell lies."

The "bwoy" (Jamaican patois for the word *boy*) he was referring to was me. The chairman promised to look into the matter. I closed my office door, and Mr. and Mrs. Neil left without any further incidents.

It was to be the beginning of many sorrows I would have to endure with Mrs. Neil during my time at Munro.

The third incident also occurred within a few days on the job. Again, I was in my office when the former acting headmaster put his head around the office door and said, "They are burning down buildings up in your country."

Having said that, he turned around and left my office without any further explanation. I later found out that what he was referring to was the 9/11 incident that was happening in New York City. But what I found interesting was what he had said, "They are burning down buildings up in your country." Now he knew that I was Jamaican by birth but had lived in the States for over twenty years. But apparently, he thought that it was much more likely that America should now be regarded as my country more so than Jamaica. It was really his way of telling me that I wasn't really welcomed. That I should think about going back to America. Interesting! It was something that I took note of and would later help to clarify for me some of the strong opposition I would later face from some members of the staff to my efforts to run a more efficient school.

Controversies

THOSE INCIDENTS COULD be regarded as being minor when compared to three major controversies that were to garner nationwide attention. These were to have a major impact on my stay at Munro.

The first major controversy erupted within a week of me being at Munro. Six new students had been transferred to the school from other schools in the capital city of Kingston. I was not involved with that decision. It was made before I got there. Within a few days of the start of school, a member of the staff saw them smoking ganja (marijuana) on the campus. Now any form of smoking was strictly prohibited, and smoking ganja was regarded as particularly serious.

Being new on the job, I sought the help of senior members of staff as to how to deal with matter and was told that such an incident was serious enough that it mandated a ten-day suspension from school and a recommendation to the school board that they be expelled. And that is what I did. Because the school board was unable to take up the matter within the ten days of the suspension, the chairman extended it for another five days until the board could meet. The board met, and the members voted overwhelmingly that the boys should be expelled.

The incident created a firestorm across the island and was covered extensively by the print media, as well as radio and television. It became an even bigger news item when the Minister of Education himself decided to overturn the board's decision after the boys appealed their suspension directly to him. The minister's decision was to cause much consternation all around. There were demonstrations at the school against his decision, and it became the main topic of discussion on talk shows for several days. The entire school board, except one person, decided to resign in protest. In the end, the boys were returned to the school, and the minister got to hand-pick those he wanted to be members of the new board.

Now in Jamaica, each school has its own individual school board. All the schools come under the direct authority of the Minister of Education. The Ministry of Education sets the broad educational policies that spell out how schools are operated. They also choose the people to be on the board. While the board does not have any input in the day-to-day operations of the school, it is their responsibility to make sure that the ministry's policies are been carried out in the school. In addition, they got to choose who is appointed principal and vice principal of the school. School boards are usual made up of people deemed to be the outstanding citizens in the area where the school is located.

At a school like Munro College, the majority of the board was usually made up of outstanding alumni or "old boys" as they were called.

So within a month of being on the job, I no longer had the members of the board that had hired me to support me. I was going to have to go forward with a new board that I did not know and who knew nothing about me. I was tempted to quit, and my wife was very much for the idea, but the outgoing chairman pleaded with me to stay.

"We brought you here because we believe that Munro needs a headmaster like you right now" were his parting words to me.

For all the time I was to remain at Munro, working with the new board was to be just one of the major challenges I would face while trying to do my job effectively. It was told to me some time later that many of the new board members would often refer to me as "Mr. Sharpe's boy," an apparent reference to the former chairman who was instrumental in my coming to Munro.

Controversy number two erupted at the start of my third year at Munro.

Students starting high school and coming to a school like Munro usually do so because they sat and passed an exam similar to the one I took back in 1964 that allowed me to go to Manning's High School. While a student can indicate a preference as to which high school they wished to attend, they might simply have gone to the one the Ministry of Education designated. A parent can contact the principal of nearby school to find out if there was any space so they could have their child transferred to that school. It was usually up to the principal to determine whether they would accept such a transfer. If the parents could not get a transfer, then the child would have to attend the high school designated for him or her to attend. Usually, the parents of a new student would have to indicate to the school whether their child was going to be attending that school or not.

A school like Munro was very unique. It was the only boarding high school for boys on the entire island. It meant that parents were much more likely to want to get their boy into Munro than to have him transferred from there. That is the reason why Munro was the only school in Jamaica that had boys from all fourteen parishes as well as six different countries. The fact that it was a boarding school made it even more attractive for parents. They knew that meant their sons would have twenty-four hours' supervision, and because of the location of the school, way out in the country, there wasn't much they could do except study and play sports.

And so it was that a young boy living in Kingston had won a scholarship to come to Munro. There were several outstanding high schools in Kingston, but they were not Munro. When she and her son turned up on campus, I noticed right away that he had his hair plaited and set on his head in what Jamaicans called "chiney bump." It is a style often worn by girls or women. At Munro, all the boys are required to be neatly groomed with their hair cut to an appropriate length. I informed the mother about the school's policy regarding hair grooming, and after she had gotten all the necessary information about what he would need to start school, she and her son left.

Imagine my surprise when I woke up the following day to a blaring headline in the newspaper that said, "Principal Refused to

Allow Boy Who Is a Rastafarian to Enroll in School." Suddenly, Munro was the center of another controversy again. Talk radio hosts and other progressives were up in arms about me wanting to deny a boy his education because he was a Rastafarian. The mother had told members of the media that I told her that the only way the boy would be allowed to come to Munro was if he cut his hair. Now nothing could have been further from the truth.

At no time during our conversation did the mother tell me or made any indication that they were Rastafarians. Even the way his hair was plaited did not indicate any such thing. All I did was to tell her about the school's policy on proper grooming for boys attending Munro. That had been the school's policy for as long as anyone could remember.

That day, the media descended on the campus like a pack of wolves to ask questions and devour who they could. I knew from a previous controversy that it was best not to make any statement before I had a chance to inform the Ministry of Education about what had happened. But before that could happen, the ministry was already issuing a statement that no child could be denied entrance to the school because of their religious beliefs. They didn't even check with me before they issued their statement.

I could tell that the whole thing had turned political and that by his statement, the minister was opening the door to having other boys turn up on campus with "natty dread" hairstyle claiming that they were Rastafarians.

I sent a message to the mother of the boy and asked her to come back and see me. When she came, I told her it was never my intention to deny her son entrance to Munro. Besides, I told her, the Ministry of Education had made it clear that that was not going to happen.

Now the minister and the ministry might have thought they had put me in my place by issuing a statement without any prior consultation with me, but there was a trump card that I as the head-master of the school held that not even the minister himself could do anything about.

While boys might have the right to come to the school, they had no right to boarding. And so, I told the mother that I was not going to offer boarding for her son. She would have to find boarding for him off campus while he attended school. It meant that after a certain time, he would have to leave the campus each day since he was not a boarder. The mother was not happy with my decision and again went and complained to the Ministry of Education and the media, but there was nothing either could do about it.

The third firestorm that erupted resulted in the entire auxiliary staff on the campus going on strike. The auxiliary staff consisted of those workers who kept the campus grounds clean, those who cleaned the boys' dorms, as well as those who worked in the canteen (cafeteria).

I had called a meeting of the auxiliary staff, and since they were unionized, it was a requirement that the union representative be present at the meeting. I had informed him of the time and location of the meeting. When the time came for the meeting, he was nowhere to be seen, and so I proceeded with the meeting. I don't recall specifically why the meeting was held, but I know it was not about anything major.

Just as I was about to wrap up the meeting, the union rep turned up, and as he was walking in, I looked up and said, "You're late, I am just about to end the meeting."

He immediately began telling me that I had no right to start without him.

"Then you should have been on time," I said.

I could see that he was getting agitated so I asked him to come with me to my office so we could talk. The meeting ended, and he and I walked over to my office. We had an amicable conversation, and we both walked out of my office together and walked across the campus still in conversation.

The following morning, before I could get dressed and go out on the campus, there was a loud knock on my door. Now I am usually out the door of the headmaster's residence by seven o'clock every morning. So that knock came much earlier than that. It was the head prefect or the head boy as they are called in schools in Jamaica. He came to tell me that the entire auxiliary staff was on strike, and therefore, no breakfast was being prepared for the boys.

"And why are they on strike?" I asked incredulously.

"Because of you, sir," he responded.

Apparently, they were upset with the way I had spoken to their union rep the day before and decided to go on strike. I had to quickly put some plans in place to get some parents from the surrounding community to come in and cook breakfast for the boys. I also asked for a meeting with the staff members, but they refused to meet with me. I was told that they had reported the matter to their union headquarters in Kingston, and they were expecting one of the vice presidents of the union to come down to investigate the matter.

After some phone calls between the chairman of the board and the union headquarters, it was decided that the workers would go back to work, and the vice president would come and talk with me. After they went back to work, I again asked that the workers meet with me, and this time, they agreed. I told them about the conversation I had with their union rep, and that when he left my office, I thought that everything was cleared up between us.

"But dat kno wha him tell wi sah" (That isn't what he told us, sir) was the response of one of the workers. Apparently, the union rep felt that I had embarrassed him in front of the workers, and even though I thought we had cleared things up between us, he still went back and lied to persuade them to strike in retaliation.

The sad thing was that this union rep was also a member of the school board that I had to deal with during my time at Munro. Those kinds of things were to weigh heavily in my eventual decision to leave Munro.

Come and Get Your Daughter

I T WAS WHILE I was in the midst of all this chaos and confusion at Munro that one morning, my secretary popped her head around the door of my office and said, "Dr. Hendricks, you have a phone call."

As she said that, I noticed that there was a sly smile on her face.

"Who is it?' I asked.

"She said she is your wife."

And then she closed the door. I immediately began wondering why Scottie would be calling me on the phone. The principal's office was right next to the library in the principal's residence, and all she would need to do is knock to see if I had anyone in my office and then come in. There was absolutely no reason for her to call me unless she had left the campus without my knowledge. I picked up the phone and said hello.

"Earl, this is Nicky, you need to come and get your daughter."

I was stunned.

It had been nearly four years since I had seen or heard from Nicky or my youngest daughter, Sara, after they had moved to New York. In fact, the last time I had heard from Nicky was the night I returned from my honeymoon and she had called to congratulate Scottie on our marriage. Scottie had firmly told her not to call our house again, and we never heard from her again. After that, I had tried various times to get in touch with her to speak with my daughter. Because I did not have a direct number for her, I had tried going through mutual friends whom we knew when we lived in New York.

I soon found out that these friends had no interest in taking my phone calls, neither were they willing to give me Nicky's number or pass on any message from me to my daughter. I soon realized that Nicky had poisoned these people's minds against me, and to them, I was a villain.

Pursuant to the divorce agreement, I had custody of Sara, and Nicky was supposed to start paying me child support for Sara. But since the child was living with her, I decided that I would send her a monthly check to help take care of our daughter. I was able to find an address for Nicky, and each month for nearly three years, I sent a check in Sara's name with a little note telling her how much I loved and missed her. Over the course of those years, not one of those checks were ever cashed. Each month as I balanced my checkbook, I would balance it as if the checks were cashed. I wanted to make sure that if Nicky ever did decide to cash those checks that the money would be in the bank to cover them. Those funds stayed in the bank until June of 2001 when I closed the account and moved to Jamaica.

I had always wondered what was going on with my daughter. Having not grown up with my parents, I had resolved that that wouldn't be the case with my own kids. I had reluctantly agreed to let Nicky take Sara to New York with her and had only agreed to it because she had begged me to allow her to go. It had never occurred to me that Nicky would then proceed to keep my daughter away from me and had done so for nearly four years. During that time, I suffered a tremendous amount of guilt. I blamed myself for agreeing to it in the first place, and now I was without the resources or any method with which to try and find Sara and get her back.

So you can imagine my utter shock when the person claiming to be my wife on the other end of the phone said, "Come and get your daughter."

Quickly getting over my shock, I asked her, "What are you talking about?"

At which point, she proceeded to remind me that I was the one who was given custody of Sara and that she no longer wanted to keep her. I was confused and at a loss as to what to do. She was in New York; I was in Jamaica. How was I going to be able to arrange to get my little girl? I asked Nicky for a number and told her I would call her back about what I intended to do. I knew though that I needed to get my baby girl as far away from Nicky as I could, but right at that moment, I had no idea how to go about doing that.

As I pondered the matter, I remembered that Sara's oldest sister, Nicole, was married and living in Atlanta, Georgia. I called her and asked her if she could get Sara until I could arrange something. It was then she suggested that I should write a letter giving her permission to take Sara on my behalf, and that way, it would be legal for Nicole to go and get Sara and that is what I did.

Sara was twelve years old at the time, just twelve years younger than Nicole. Nicole had recently married a Jamaican fellow and had moved to Jamaica for a while before moving back to Atlanta. Despite being virtual newlyweds, with no kids of their own, Nicole and her husband opened their home and hearts to Sara and raised her as if she was their own child. In fact, when I returned to the States to live, Sara was doing so well with Nicole that I let her continue living with her while she completed high school and college. Rarely did Nicole ever call me to ask for any financial help for Sara. Incredibly, she did virtually all of it on her own.

It was several years after that phone call from Nicky that I was to find out what led up to her calling me that day to "Come and get your daughter." Apparently, for all those four years, Nicky had been feeding Sara with all sorts of untrue stories about me. These ranged from I was dead to I had abandoned her and her mother. So Sara was growing up thinking that she did not have a father. As I was led to understand it, everything changed one day when Sara went in the closet at her mother's apartment to get something, and a shoe box fell down and out fell all the checks that I had sent that her mother had refused to cash. Sara, on seeing this, became very angry and very rebellious after that, to the extent that her mother felt that she could no longer control her. What was ironic was after Sara went to live with her sister, she exhibited none of those same rebellious habits. According to Nicole, as she grew up and went through high school, she was a model student, who graduated among the top students in her class and went on to university and law school. Sara is now a married mother of two living in Atlanta.

Just to be clear, after that initial phone call with Nicky, I made it a point to explain to my secretary that the phone call was not from my wife but my ex-wife. I believe Nicky had deliberately told her that because she probably thought that was some way, she could create some mischief for me. As I reflect on all this, I shudder to think what might have become of my baby girl if she had had to continue living with her mother. I remain incredibly grateful for Nicole's willingness to step in and care for Sara during that difficult time.

Just Common Sense

I WAS SOON to find out that many of the decisions that were needed for a more efficient functioning of the school were just things that required some common sense. Why those decisions had not been made in the past was beyond me. I remember having a conversation with the headmistress of Hampton High School for girls that was located about three miles away and was regarded as the sister school for Munro. It was common practice between the two schools to have sixth form students take advanced classes at the school that offered them. So it was not uncommon to see girls from Hampton on the campus at Munro and for there to be boys from Munro on the campus at Hampton.

During one of our conversation, I had asked her, "How is it that Hampton, which is a girls' school and located on a considerably less amount of land than Munro, was winning national awards in agriculture and Munro, a boy's school, wasn't? Why is that?"

Her answer floored me.

"Dr. Hendricks, "she said, "Hampton functions!"

Hampton functions! I guess that about summed it up.

One of the many complaints that I had to deal with at the beginning of the school year was that some of the boys would often stay on the dorms instead of going to class. Boys were supposed to be out of their dormitories and ready to go to breakfast by 6:30 in the morning. After breakfast and a school assembly, classes would start around 8:30. Many of the boys would then go back and hide out in the dorms and miss their classes. My simple solution was when the boys left the dorms in the morning that the ladies who clean the dorms should lock the doors so that they couldn't get back in. It was a simple solution that worked.

The dorms themselves were not very attractive. There were just large rooms with bunk beds. I thought we could make them more livable if we hung curtains on the windows and put up mirrors throughout the dorm so the boys could see themselves as they got dressed.

Water was also a problem. The school used tanks to collect rainwater for use on the campus. But there were times when water had to be pumped onto the campus to fill up the tanks. The headmaster's house had its own tank, and when enough rain did not fall to fill it up, water would then have to be trucked in. It took seven trips to fill the tank. When I checked the cost of each trip and compared it to the cost of running a pipe from the main tank to the headmaster's tank so that when water was pumped to the main tank, some could also go to that tank, I found that the one-time cost for doing so came as the cost of the seven trips that the trucks had to make. So by spending that amount of money just once, we would never have to do so again, and the headmaster's house would never again be without water.

It was terrible to watch the boys slipping and sliding and falling in the mud every time it rained. There were certain parts of the campus that were high traffic areas, and these were the areas that were particularly troublesome when it rained. The solution was to have outdoor nonslip tiles put down that would allow the boys to get around the campus without the fear of falling every time it rained. And so, I had nonslip tiles strategically laid around the main parts of the campus to facilitate easy moving around, even when it rained.

Agricultural science was one of the subjects taught. It was not, however, one of the main or core subjects. It was highly unlikely that a boy came to Munro with the thought of going into farming. It was not impossible but highly unlikely. The sciences, however, were a different thing. Science was a major focus of the school. Imagine my surprise when I found out that the teacher for agricultural science had the top floor of a relatively new building that he used to only store his tools. Meanwhile, the teachers of subjects like biology and physics only had a little hole-in-the-wall space for their most important subjects. I made sure that that inequity was corrected and moved biology and physics to the larger space and told the teacher of agricultural science that he could have the hole-in-the-wall.

This person had been at the school for nearly thirty years and was most unhappy with my decision, but I really didn't care. The school had not shown any growth in the area of agriculture, even though it was located on nearly two hundred acres of land, had a farm, and some livestock. Since it was a boarding school, I was surprise to find out that very little of the ground provisions that was needed to feed the boys was being grown on the farm. It was a waste of money and space.

The school had nearly seven hundred students. About a half of them lived on campus while the others were bused to and from school each day. The school had signed an exclusive contract with a bus company to provide this service. Under the terms of the contract, the school was to pay the bus company a sum of about a quarter million dollars (Jamaican) every two weeks. It then became the school's responsibility to recoup that money from the parents of the boys who rode the buses. This was much easier said than done. And so, the school was always paying out money that it was having quite a problem getting back.

Soon after I arrived, the contract was up for renewal, and I informed the owner of the bus company that I was quite willing to renew the contract for the previous amount or more if that was what he decided but with one stipulation. He would now be responsible for collecting the money from the parents himself. As much as he could see that it was going to create some difficulties for him, he readily agreed, and once again, the school was able to save some much-needed funds.

With seven hundred boys on campus, feeding them each day was no small feat. The school provided three meals each day for the boarders and lunch for those who were bused to school. Those three meals were hardly going to be enough for growing boys. It was also highly unlikely that all the boys were going to be satisfied with what was being offered in the canteen (cafeteria) each day. The fact that the school was located some distance from the nearest store and leaving the campus was strictly forbidden meant that they were stuck with what was available on campus.

In order to help with that problem there was a tuck shop, a place that offered the boys some other choices of food like patties, coco bread, sodas, and other baked products. They could also purchase things like toothpaste and toilet tissue. It meant that each day, the boys were spending hundreds if not thousands of dollars buying these things at the tuck shop. The problem was the school did not control the tuck shop. Someone was paying the school a minuscule amount each month to operate the tuck shop on campus. Again, as soon as I could, I had the school take charge of running the tuck shop, expanded what it provided, and within the first three months of doing that, it was showing net profit of more than a half a million dollars (Jamaican).

In Jamaica, a student can attend high school for up to seven years. The first five years are considered as the regular years. Years six and seven though are for those students who have done exceptionally well on their fifth-year exams and can go on to do advanced studies that prepare them for entrance to the university. In your first year in high school, you are placed in first form. In your second year, you go onto second form and so on until you get to fifth form, and if you qualify for your sixth year, you go to lower six form and for your seventh to upper six.

Each form at Munro consisted of three groups consisting of about thirty to thirty-five boys. I realized from my experience teaching at a magnet school in America that it was much easier for a teacher to effectively teach and manage a smaller class than a big one. Thirty to thirty-five students in a class was just too much. And so, I expanded the groups for the first three years at Munro to four instead of three. It meant that the most a teacher would have in a group of students would be twenty to twenty-five boys. This was a much more manageable number than before. As the students advanced in their years in school, they would have the same number of groups all the way through fifth form.

The school bursar was the person responsible for keeping check on all the money that came to and was spent by the school. Each month, she would meet with me to bring me up-to-date on the status of the school's finances. In one of our first meeting, she told me that the school had about six different bank accounts. Since money could not be comingled, different accounts had been established to ensure that funds were being used for their specific purposes. We had all these accounts at one bank, Scotia Bank. She also told me that bank fees for all the accounts were totaling nearly a million dollars (Jamaican) annually. I knew that had to change, and so I called the manager of the bank to ask for a meeting to discuss with her what could be done about those exorbitant fees.

When she came to see me and I asked about her bank's fees, her response was that there was nothing she could do about it. Now I had informed her before she came to see me specifically what I wanted to talk to her about. She traveled the approximate twenty miles from her bank just to tell me there was nothing that could be done. I thanked her and she left.

I immediately called another bank, Royal Bank of Trinidad and Tobago (RBTT), which was located only three miles from the school and asked if I could come in and speak to the manager. A date was set for the appointment, and I went in to see the manager. I told her that I was looking to move the school's various accounts but wanted to know if her bank could accommodate us without the excessive fees. She agreed to cancel all their fees if I would move our accounts to her bank, and that is what I did. The only account that remained at Scotia Bank was the account into which the Ministry of Education deposited the teachers' salaries each month. To move that account, I would need permission from the ministry, and based on my history with them, I knew it wasn't going to be forthcoming.

Now in Jamaica, parents have to pay school fees for the children going to school. These fees are to be paid into a bank account specifically set up to receive those payments. One of the problems with the previous bank was that they were not providing the school with timely update on the account. So we had no way of knowing which parents were being diligent in their payments or not. The new bank promised that they would make it a priority to get us weekly updates.

When I left Munro and returned to the States after two and half years, the school had a budget surplus of more than eight million dollars (Jamaican). That had never happened before in the history of Munro College.

It is interesting to note that just like when I had to change the length of each class from half an hour to one hour at the beginning the school year, none of the changes that I made were made without much protesting that it couldn't or shouldn't be done. The funny thing was that after the changes were implemented and were proving to be very successful, none of the protestors, including members of the school board, ever came back to say that they were wrong.

Years later, I would return to Munro to visit some friends and was to see that many of the things I had suggested to be done and did not receive any support for were in fact now done and in place.

The Infamous Mrs. Sonia Neil

I HADN'T SEEN or heard from Mrs. Neil after she barged into my office and accused me of wanting to cane her son and her husband threatened to do me bodily harm if I had done so. I was told that she was to be away for the entire time from September to December and would be returning to her position as vice principal come January of the new year.

As I have mentioned before, I knew Mrs. Neil from our time at teachers' college, but we were not friends and I knew very little about her personally. During my many conversations with the headmistress of Hampton School, I was able to get additional information about Mrs. Neil.

Mrs. Neil had been a teacher at Hampton for many years. But when the headmistress she was working with resigned and the school board chose the current headmistress for the position instead of someone Mrs. Neil felt should have been chosen, she too resigned her position at Hampton in protest. She ended up at Munro as a teacher of Spanish. After a couple years at Munro, she had the distinction of being chosen the first female vice principal in the history of the school.

After being in that position for a number of years, when the post of headmaster became available again, Mrs. Neil applied for it but was turned down. The board felt that it was only appropriate that a boarding school for boys have a man as the headmaster.

It was after she found out that I had been appointed as the new headmaster that she decided to take a leave of absence to further her studies. In one of my conversations with the headmistress of Hampton, she had also relayed some things I found very telling. She told me that she had been hesitant to be too accepting of me when I first arrived because of something Mrs. Neil had told her about me when it was first announced that I was coming Munro. In talking to Mrs. Neil about my appointment to Munro, Mrs. Neil's response was "Earl Hendricks, I know Earl Hendricks, and he isn't going to amount to much." Wow! Imagine that!

Here was someone who knew absolutely nothing about me, had never had a single conversation with me, did not know what I had been up to in the nearly thirty years since we both graduated teachers' college, and yet she was now making the most definitive statements about me and my abilities and was already certain that I was going to fail in my new position at Munro.

Mrs. Neil did not know that her conversation had been shared with me, and I never let on that I knew about it. The headmistress admitted that she had only decided to share it with me after she heard how the Neils had behaved when they came to see me at the beginning of the school year. She also told me that after working closely with me on matters affecting both schools, as well as another local prep school that was a feeder school for both our schools, she realized that I was, in fact, a very hardworking person with a clear vision as to where I wanted to take Munro.

It was armed with that background information that I was to begin working with the infamous Mrs. Sonia Neil in the coming calendar year.

The first day of school in the new calendar year began as usual with the boarders arriving the weekend before and getting settled in their dorms. That Monday morning, all the other students arrived. I was out on the campus as usual to supervise things and make sure that everything was in order. I didn't know or observe when Mrs. Neil arrived on the campus. I only found out when I saw her in the auditorium where everyone had come for the regular weekly headmaster's assembly. After the assembly, she headed straight for her office without saying a word to me.

When Mrs. Neil arrived for the new term, she also found that she had a new secretary. She probably knew it before she got back because it was common knowledge that they were very close friends. Her new secretary was my former secretary. I had decided to find a new secretary and decided to move her downstairs to be with her friend, Mrs. Neil. My decision was based on the fact that after the Neils' visit to my office, the chairman had followed up to investigate like he promised. My former secretary was among the people he spoke with. She was seated in her office just outside the door to my office when everything was happening. When she was asked to relay what she had seen and heard, she told the chairman she had not seen or heard anything. It was then that I realized that I was never going to be able to trust her, and if she remained as my secretary, she was probably going to be relaying everything that was said in my office back to Mrs. Neil.

It was later on that I realized that sending her down to Mrs. Neil was probably not a good idea, as the two of them would conspire to try and put as many roadblocks in my way as they possibly could.

Mrs. Neil and I were never able to see eye to eye during my time at Munro. It became obvious to me that one of her problems had to do with the fact that she had to address me as Dr. Hendricks. She had somehow convinced herself that she was more than my equal in intelligence. In fact, on one occasion, she made it a point to very forcefully say to me, "I am a very intelligent woman, Dr. Hendricks."

To which I just as forcefully responded, "But not as intelligent as I am, Mrs. Neil."

I was never one to brag, but on that occasion, I had to let her know that I was not at all impressed with her shenanigans.

That was why she was so desperate to complete her masters' degree at the University of the West Indies. But even then, she knew that she would still not be called doctor, and it was obvious that it galled her that I was and she wasn't.

My final experience with Mrs. Neil before I left Munro was typical of the woman. I had announced that I was not coming back after the Christmas term. And it so happened that the headmistress at Hampton had also announced that she was resigning her position as well. She had announced it much earlier than I did, so as the term went on, they had already begun to interview people to fill her position. And sure enough, one of the people applying to replace her was none other than Mrs. Sonia Neil.

Now mark you, this is the same Sonia Neil who several years before had resigned her teaching position at Hampton because she was unhappy about the appointment of the new headmistress instead of her personal friend whom she thought was more deserving. Not only had she resigned but she had made it her duty to go and inform the new headmistress that she did not think she deserved the position. It was this same headmistress position that Mrs. Neil was now applying to fill.

Mrs. Neil was among those that were invited to be interviewed, but what she didn't know was that the panel responsible for choosing the new headmistress also included the current headmistress. I can only imagine how surprised and shocked she must have been when she walked into the interview and realized that the same person whom she had so flippantly dismissed as undeserving several years ago was going to be the same one helping to determine who would succeed her as headmistress at Hampton High School for girls.

Mrs. Neil was not chosen. Among the reasons shared with me by the outgoing headmistress was that Mrs. Neil had applied for the position without including any reference from the principal of the school where she was the vice principal. The panel thought it was strange that she did not feel that she could have asked for and get a good recommendation from her current employer. In fact, Mrs. Neil had not informed me of her decision to apply for the position of headmistress at Hampton. She also did not ask me for a letter of recommendation. Apparently, she didn't think she needed one. The people making the decision thought differently.

Another thing that apparently worked against her was when she was asked about her vision for the school, she responded that her vision was the same as the current headmistress. The current headmistress sitting there was shocked and bewildered since she had never shared any of her vision with Mrs. Neil nor had they had any conversation about such matters. And again, what was so silly was that she was claiming the same vision as the person whom she had once derided as not being good enough to be the headmistress. That didn't make any sense to me and neither to the people making the decision.

And so, when I left Munro, Mrs. Neil was still entombed downstairs in her little office space below the headmaster's very large office. When a new headmaster was to be chosen for Munro College, she was once again passed over.

It was several years after I had returned to the States that I was informed that she had died.

Objectives Met

THE MAIN OBJECTIVE, with which I was charged when I was hired as headmaster at Munro, was to help return the school to one of academic excellence again. That became my primary goal.

I remember having a conversation with one of the boys in upper six soon after I arrived at Munro, and he wanted to know why I would give up what he considered my life of comfort in America to come back to Jamaica. He said to me that things were not good in Jamaica and that discipline in the schools was particularly bad.

"Why would you want to come back to this?" he asked.

I told him that I had always wanted to come back to give something back to my country. I then shared with him some of my plans to help return the school to one of academic excellence again.

"And how long do you think that is going to take?" he asked.

"Five years," I said.

When I arrived at Munro, only thirty-two boys from that year's fifth form had done well enough to go on to lower six. To be promoted to lower six, a student had to have passed at least five subjects with distinctions from their fifth form exams. That year, fifth form had one hundred and twenty-five boys. That only thirty-two had done well enough to go on to lower six was just not good enough. Apparently, that was the kind of results the school had been experiencing for several years. It was no wonder that the chairman of the school board was so concerned about the school's academic performance.

At the beginning of my third year at Munro, of the one hundred and twenty-five boys who took their fifth form exam, seventy-two were able to go on to lower six. It meant that in two years, we were able to increase the percentage of boys who went on to do advance studies in sixth form from 25 percent of fifth formers to 60 percent.

Going to sixth form was particularly important for those students who wanted to go on to university. Students who had an interest in studying in areas like medicine, business, or even law would greatly benefit from the solid foundation obtained by doing the two years of advance work in high school before they went on to university. Successful completion of the two years in sixth form made future acceptance into the university an almost certainty. That is why only those students with passes with distinctions in at least five subjects were able to go to sixth form.

That year, there were also about fifteen other boys who had four passes with distinctions, and so we established a new form level just below lower six, where they were allowed to start doing some advanced studies while they work on getting the one additional subject with distinction that they would need to be fully accepted in the sixth form. It meant that for that year, we had a total of nearly ninety students who were doing advanced studies beyond fifth form.

It didn't stop there. When the results were published for all the high schools on the island in passes in English, math, and the sciences, Munro was ranked fourth in the entire island. The only schools ranked above Munro were two high schools for girls and another high school for boys in Kingston. I remember the new chairman of the school board calling me to inquire whether those results could possibly be true. I assured him that these result were very much true.

Another of my objectives was to restore the high level of discipline to the school. I would tell the boys that when it came to discipline, I was as cold as steel and merciless as an executioner. That particular saying was to get me reported to the Ministry of Education. They were told that I was threatening to do the boys bodily harm.

It would not be the only time that the Ministry of Education would receive an anonymous complaint from Munro about me. One of the things I did was develop a mantra for the boys to repeat each time they gathered for the headmaster's assembly on Monday mornings. It was the same mantra that I would later adopt for the Avenue D Boys' Choir. When I first developed the mantra, the first line said, "We are young black men of honor."

Now at the time, out of a student body of over seven hundred students, only two were white. But someone wrote to the ministry to complain that I was excluding students at Munro because of the color of their skin. To avoid any confusion, I dropped the word *black* and made it so that it read, "We are young men of honor, pursuing excellence and leading by example."

That mantra became so popular that parents were asking that it become the motto of the school. One senior teacher, who would later leave Munro to become a headmaster himself, adopted it for his new school. And later, it was to receive international recognition as the mantra of the famous Avenue D Boys' Choir.

There were two incidents that happened that made it clear to me that Munro's reputation for discipline was becoming well-known.

The first occurred while I was hurriedly on my way to Kingston one day. In my haste, I attempted to overtake a car around a corner, only to run into a police roadblock. They pulled me over and asked for my license and insurance. When I handed the police officer my license, he took one look at it and said, "You are the Dr. Hendricks that I have heard so much about?"

"I am," I said.

"Well, sir," he said. "I hear what a great disciplinarian you are. Maybe you should start applying that same discipline to your driving."

With that, he handed me back my license and sent me on my way.

At another time, I was in the green room at the television station waiting to go on to be interviewed when a lady walked in and sat down. I didn't say anything to her, and she did not speak to me. After a while, a television staff member came out and said, "Dr. Hendricks, you will be going on in five minutes."

"Thanks," I said.

After the staff member left, the lady looked up at me and asked, "You are the Dr. Hendricks from Munro College?"

"Yes," I said, wondering why she asked.

The lady got up, came over to me, bowed, and said, "My respect to you, sir," and then went and sat down.

It's Time to Go

THE TWO AND a half years I spent at Munro were not easy for me. For one thing, my wife continued to be unhappy with her life in Jamaica. It didn't help that some of her jewelry had been stolen by someone who was doing some renovation work on the headmaster's house. Since we had a house manager, there was very little for her to do in the house. She didn't have to cook, clean, wash, or iron my clothes. All of those tasks were being done for us, and so she would sit in the house all day, having absolutely nothing to do.

Since I knew she had a love of music and a talent for singing, I suggested she consider starting a choir at Munro. She jumped at the idea, and at one time, she had about seventy boys in the choir. When the time for the annual festival celebration came around, she entered her boys' choir in the festival competition for gospel choirs. For two years in a row, the boys' choir from Munro College won the award for the most outstanding gospel choir on the island.

My wife, being able to find her niche at the school, allowed her to develop some lasting relationships with some of the boys that have continued to this day, but it did not do much to alleviate the many other challenges that I was facing.

It was always a huge problem to get anything done for the school on a timely basis. It was as if there were people at the Ministry of Education and the school board who were constantly trying to put roadblocks in my way.

169

Every year, I would request desks for the school from the Ministry of Education. And in two years, they provided me with only twenty new desks. It meant that we constantly had to be scrambling to find old desks that we could patch up so the boys could have desks in their classrooms.

It was my understanding that in its more than one-hundred-and-fifty-year history, the school had never been audited. And yet within a few months of me being there, a team from the Ministry of Education descended on the campus to do an audit.

Apparently, someone had sent an anonymous tip to the ministry that the headmaster was using the school's money for his personal use. The allegations were not true, but someone from the Ministry of Education felt that they needed to come to investigate by doing a complete audit.

What happened was that the former board that hired me had purchased a new car for the headmaster's use. I had nothing to do with the decision to purchase the vehicle, and I certainly had not spent a dime of the school's funds to purchase it. The car was purchased as the property of the school for my use, but it was not mine personally. The auditors had questions about the purchase of the car which the former chairman could easily have answered if they had bothered to give him a call. They didn't.

I was never to find out what else they needed to know about the school's operations since they never spoke to me at all, and I was never able to see a copy of the audit or any report that they had supposedly done.

As time went on, I was becoming more and more frustrated with the situation. The school itself was doing extremely well. Not only were there incredible improvements in academics, in the time I was there, the school had won the nationwide school challenge competition among all the island's high schools. This was a competition that measured students' knowledge about a wide range of subjects. It was modeled on the very popular game show *Jeopardy* in the United States. Munro also finished second in the annual debate competition among high schools in Jamaica. But despite all these successes, there were always concerted efforts to make my job and my life as difficult and as miserable as possible.

The school was not able to win any national sport championship, and to some people, winning a national sport championship was far more important than the school's outstanding academic achievements.

The final straw for me occurred at the beginning of my third year at the school. Two boys were caught fighting on campus with knives. We had never had an incident like that before, and it was regarded as being very serious. I carried out an investigation of the incident, being careful to follow the education handbook guidelines provided by the Ministry of Education.

According to the guidelines, when a serious disciplinary incident happened on a school campus, the headmaster (or principal) should investigate, write a report, give the students involved a ten-day suspension if the incident was serious enough, and send a written report to the chairman of the school board. I did all of that and recommended to the board that I thought the incident was serious enough to warrant the expulsion of the boys involved.

I waited for nearly two weeks and heard nothing from the chairman of the board. Notably, after the ten-day suspension; if the board hadn't acted, the boys would have to be returned to school. And so, I called the chairman to find out what was going on and was told that he and the vice chairman were coming to the school to investigate the matter in a few days. I told him I would be sure to make myself available.

"Oh no," he said. "You won't be involved anymore."

"And why is that?" I asked.

"Well," he said, "you have already made your recommendation, so we won't need anything further from you."

I was shocked. I had never heard of anything happening like that before, but there was nothing else I felt I could do. And so they came and had their investigation without any further involvement from me.

While I was surprised that they didn't want me in their meeting, I was flabbergasted when I got a letter from the chairman with his written report and recommendations. First of all, he told me in his letter that the delay in the board's investigation of the matter was because I had dropped the ball. His recommendations were that I should have the boys return to school, cane them, and put them on probation.

Well, first of all, I had not dropped the ball, as he asserted. He and the board were the people who had done so, not me and I told him so in my written response to his letter. I also suggested that since they had made their decision without considering my recommendation, that he or some other member of the board should also come and do the caning of the boys. That really ticked him off. He was livid that I could suggest such a thing. But by this time, I had stopped caring about what these people thought. He was not the only one capable of being ticked off; I was too at his blatant attempt to pass the buck because of his and the board's obvious incompetence.

I had followed the ministry's guidelines to the letter, and the fact of the matter was that it was their failure to deal with the matter in a timely manner that resulted in the only alternative being that the boys had to be returned to school without any further punishment since their ten-day suspension had expired before the board made their decision.

It was not the first time that the chairman had acted in a way that proved to me that he was just behaving antagonistically toward me. In July 2003, he sent me a letter confirming my permanent appointment as headmaster of Munro. The problem was the Ministry of Education had made that decision effective September of the prior year, but I was only now being informed of it some ten months later.

It was situations like those that helped me make up my mind that it was time to leave. And so, at the next school board meeting, after I had made my oral report on the school's operations, I announced that I was leaving at the end of that calendar year. My wife was ecstatic when I told her we were going home.

A few days before I left Munro, a teacher handed me a note that read: "To two excellent parents: I thought that when you left, a part of me would leave with you: That part that always wanted to work for excellence. I've listened as your words changed that thought. That part that always worked for excellence is the part of you that will stay with me."

I still have that note and treasure it to this very day.

And so it was that on December 18, 2003, after nearly two and half years at Munro College, my wife and I returned to resume our lives in the United States.

Why I Left Munro College

WHEN I FIRST announced that I would be leaving Munro, the news took everyone by surprise. About a week after the announcement, approximately three hundred parents converged on the campus to find out why. The question most frequently on their lips was "Why are you leaving?" Most of the time, my standard response was that I felt that it was time for my wife and I to return to the States to resume our lives.

But I always knew that there was going to come a time when I was going to have to give a written explanation for my decision to leave Munro College. The reasons fall under all the categories or all the stakeholders associated with education at Munro. The Ministry of Education, the Board of Trustees, the Board of Governors, the staff members, the students, and other intangibles.

Let me begin with the Ministry of Education. Education in Jamaica did not seem to be a priority at all for this ministry. In the two years I spent at Munro College, we only received a total of fifty desks and chairs from the Ministry of Education. It was bad enough that schools were being asked to do so much with so little resources, but when the basic resources that were needed, like desks and chairs, were not provided, then the lack of any other resources became irrelevant. For instance, I was made aware that there were at least four classes at a nearby high school that had no desks or chairs for the students. At Munro, we were constantly trying to locate old desks and chairs to repair in order to ensure that students had something to sit on in the classrooms. And we had to do this from the annual amount of $20,000 (JA) that the Ministry of Education gave us for maintenance. That was the equivalent of $10–12,000 US dollars at the time.

In a way, I found it ironically amusing when, after the last election, the then-Minister of Finance, Dr. Omar Davis, bragged about how he spent government dollars to help win the election for his party, and schools did not have even the basic resources like desks and chairs. So despite their big talk about education, I did not see any priority in terms of commitment of resources given to education in Jamaica.

The one positive thing that the Ministry of Education did in the twenty years prior to my arrival at Munro was to decentralize the ministry and establish regional offices. But even that good common-sense step had become bogged down with these regional offices becoming mini bureaucracies where very little is accomplished; lots of meetings were held, lots of reports were requested, and it was very difficult to even get a phone call returned from anyone in those offices. Sometimes, months would go by, and no one from the regional office would take the time to come and visit the school site.

In the time I spent at Munro College, I was unable to determine the purpose of the Board of Trustees that governs both Munro College and Munro Prep School. I attended several trust meetings and all that occurred were reports provided by the principals of both schools and relevant discussions regarding the items in those reports. I did not hear any articulation of any long-term strategies or goals originating from the trust to develop or maintain the schools. On several occasions, I suggested that the trust should seek to establish an endowment fund to ensure the financial viability of the schools in the future. No steps were ever taken to establish that fund.

I heard several people speak about the stalwart service that some members of the Board of Trustees had given over the years, and I kept asking myself, where is the evidence? What was the tangible proof that any service was rendered other than names on a register?

The Munro-Dickenson Trust, as far as I could tell, existed in name only. The land on which the schools are built might be trust land, but that is about all that the trust had as assets. To me, the trust's focus should not be in how the schools functioned, that should be the priority of the Board of Governors. The trust should be ensuring the future continuity of the school by making sure that there were finances available for infrastructural changes, especially in light of the government's inability to provide the necessary funds to accomplish this. When I was there, the physical plant at Munro College desperately needed a face-lift. And this was not done—indeed could not be done—because while it should have been the number one priority of the steward of the property, the trust, it had no plan in place to accomplish that. The trust had therefore become nothing but an empty shell with much rhetoric and very little substance. The similarity in this instance between the government and the trust was not to be missed.

The school board was the body that was most intimately associated with the everyday operation of the school and yet the board met only once per term, and here again the main function at those meetings was the report of the principal. There were times when I reported a situation affecting the school to the chairman of the board before a scheduled board meeting, and no action was ever taken. Board meetings were always held at a frantic (rush-through) mode. Members of the board were always in a hurry to get back to some other matters of concern to them on the day of the scheduled meetings. I do not recall a single time that any member of the board, other than Dr. Paul Auden and Mr. Keith Bell, ever took the time to just simply come by and walk the campus, talk to the students and staff members, and see what was going on.

As with the trust, on numerous occasions, I suggested that necessary steps should be taken to establish an endowment plan for the school, but to no avail. I spent several weeks putting together a student manual and a staff handbook and provided it to the board for final approval in April 2002. Up until the time I left, some twenty months later, I still had not received any notification of approval. For nearly a year, I waited for members of the board to follow up on actions needed to establish a new computer laboratory and convert an existing building on campus into administrative offices and still nothing. I will not even mention anything about the plans I suggested for reroofing and repainting some of the dormitories.

While one might not expect the board members to be actively involved in the everyday administration of the school, it should certainly be responsive to immediate concerns expressed by the principal, and the chairman of the board should be prepared, at least once in a while, to take the time to visit the school simply to let his presence be known. And because of the lack attention, areas of concern were left unaddressed by the board.

There is no doubt that there were some outstanding teachers at Munro when I was there. Among them were teachers like Ms. Noelle Hoskins, Ms. Esther Mead, Mrs. Audrey Reid, and Mr. Brian McLean, to name a few. These were by no means the only outstanding teachers that served at Munro while I was there. But there was also no doubt in my mind that one of the greatest hindrances to progress at Munro College was the person who held the position of vice principal.

Here was a person who was big on ambition, but totally lacking when it came to ability. This person was totally devoid of vision and foresight and yet was petty and childish and divisive, often creating dissension simply because she did not get her way.

Here was a person who taught at Hampton Girls' School for nearly fifteen years and at Munro College for ten years, had been vice principal at Munro and once acted as principal and yet was not considered for the position of principal at Hampton School when that position became open. The reason given, according to someone in the know, was her lack of vision and her failure to show any tangible contribution to a community where she resided for nearly thirty years. Her petty antics and unprofessional behavior at Munro had also become well-known throughout the community.

Here was a person who did nothing at Munro but sit in her office all day, never once taking the time to articulate anything that could be used to upgrade the school, never taking the time to find out what was going on in the classrooms, in the kitchen, in the dorms, or anywhere on the campus. She had absolutely no clue about anything, but loved to be seen and recognized simply because she was the vice principal.

In addition, there were other members of staff, including one teacher who had been at Munro for nearly thirty years, whose conduct could only be described as coarse and uncouth. It should not be surprising that this teacher's main area of expertise had to do with dealing with animals because that was often how this teacher behaved.

The students were perhaps among the few positive things that I came across at Munro College. Some of the most academically gifted boys I have ever encountered in all my years in education were students at Munro. These students were crying out for strong, firm, exemplary leadership, and I sought to provide that to them. The trouble was that many of the other members of staff who were to follow my lead chose not to either because they did not want to or because they simply could not. Many chose to be like the students, instead of setting the example (tone) for the students to follow. Many wanted to be liked by the students and then they would come to me to express disgust when those same students showed a lack of respect for them. Respect was not something that I had to squeeze out of the students. They saw the way I conducted myself, the way I dressed, and how visible I was about the school. They knew that I practiced what I preached. However, some teachers just did not get it. They probably were good teachers once, but there certainly was no evidence of it at the time I was getting ready to leave. I felt a great sense of sorrow for such teachers. They had been practicing their mediocre behavior for so long that they had become incapable of any semblance of excellence. In the end, the students suffered because there was very little that I, as the principal, could do to get rid of those parasites.

Finally, I left Jamaica with a tremendous sense of sadness as to where the country was going. There were times when there did not seem to be any purpose to most people's lives. They just seemed to be barely hanging on, trying to survive. And the Jamaican government certainly did not articulate any clear vision as to where it wanted to take the nation so it could grow and succeed. So Jamaica, once the pearl of the Caribbean, was fast becoming a mere sinking stone. That for me was a very sad state of affairs.

A Good Thing, but Not a God Thing

BEFORE I DECIDED to leave Munro and return to the States, I had already began making inquiries about job opportunities back in America.

I had taken a huge hit in pay when I took the job in Jamaica. I was only making about a third of what I was making as a classroom teacher in Florida. In addition, even though I was one of only three high school principals in Jamaica with a doctoral degree, I was being paid the lowest salary of all the principals on the island. A principal's salary was based on the number of students in the school, and of all the high schools on the island, Munro had the smallest student body, and so I was therefore paid accordingly. It didn't matter that the school was the only boarding high school for boys that required twenty-four-hour supervision. No, they were going strictly by their guidelines, and that was that.

When we arrived back in the States in December of 2003, I already had an appointment set up to be interviewed for a position of principal of an elementary school in Thomasville, Georgia. I had visited the town of Thomasville several times before and really liked the place. I had also met on several occasions with the superintendent of schools for Thomasville, and she had indicated to me that the interview was only a formality since she had already decided to recommend that I be appointed to the position. Unfortunately, this was January, and I would not be taking up my appointment until June. I needed a job in the meantime.

After we moved back to Florida, I remembered something that the vice principal of the school where I was teaching before I left for Jamaica said to me. He told me, "Dr. Hendricks, if you ever come back to Florida and I am the principal of a school, be sure to let me know because I would love to have you on my staff." He knew of my outstanding reputation on the campus as an outstanding teacher and classroom manager.

On one occasion, I was walking down the hallway of the school when a female teacher approached me and asked, "Are you Dr. Hendricks?"

"Yes, I am."

"I want to know," she said, "what is this effect you have on my students."

She saw the puzzled look on my face. She was a teacher at the grade level above the one I taught.

"Every time something happens in my class, all I am hearing is 'Dr. Hendricks said this and Dr. Hendricks said that.' You must be some special kind of teacher!"

I smiled with relief as I resumed walking down the hallway. I wasn't certain where she was going with her initial question.

I found out that the gentleman who had made that promise to me was now the principal of a middle school and so I went to see him. He hired me on the spot. And so it was that when the new school term began in January 2004, I had a job as a middle school teacher while I waited for June to come. My wife still had not decided whether she wanted to return to her old profession in mortgage banking and so she would drop me off to school each morning and came and picked me up in the afternoon.

After the interview in Thomasville, the superintendent told me that I would receive confirmation in the mail of my appointment. And so, we went back to Florida and waited. February came and I did not receive any such confirmation. The months of March and April came and went and still no communication. Finally, as we were approaching the end of the school year and I still had not received my letter of confirmation, I presumed they had changed their mind about it.

Then one afternoon, after I got home from school, I was shocked when I received a phone call from the superintendent. She wanted to know when I planned to arrive in Thomasville. I told her I hadn't heard from her since January and had assumed that she had changed her mind about offering me the position.

She was shocked and asked if I had not received my letter of confirmation.

"No," I said.

She told me she had given it to her secretary and asked her to have it mailed to me from January. When she went and checked, she found out the secretary still had the letter on her desk."

Dr. Hendricks," she said, "I am going to fire her."

She went on to explain that every arrangement had already been made for my arrival, including an announcement in the newspaper. They had changed the sign outside the school and had printed new letterheads for the school to include my name.

"I thought everything was in order, and we were just waiting for you to inform us when you would be arriving," she said.

I assured her that I was still excited about coming to Thomasville and would send her a date for my arrival as soon as the school year ended in Florida. When I got off the phone, I shared with my wife my conversation with the superintendent.

The following morning, she took me to school as usual. When she came to pick me up that afternoon, I noticed that she was not her usual chipper self.

"Is something wrong?" I asked.

"I have something to tell you," she said.

She had my attention.

"I spent the entire day praying about us going to Thomasville, and I am convinced I heard the Lord says that while it is a good thing, it is not a God thing and I don't think this is what we should do."

I was speechless.

My wife is not the sort of person who just goes around all willy-nilly talking about "the Lord said." I trust her judgment completely, and if she says she thinks the Lord is saying that we shouldn't go to Thomasville, I listen.

"Then we won't go," I said.

Now it was the superintendent's turn to be shocked when I informed her that I was not in fact going to take the position of principal at that elementary school. She expressed her disappointment and wished me well.

Choosing not to take that position in Thomasville meant a huge loss of income for me. I was going to be making about twice what I was currently making as a classroom teacher. But in choosing to obey the Lord's directive on that occasion as well as on others would prove the faithfulness of the Lord to us time and time again.

A Call from Jamaica

IT WAS NOT too many months after we returned from Jamaica that my phone rang, and when I looked at the number, I could tell that the call originated in Jamaica. Even though the number was not familiar to me, I still had family living on the island and there were new friends that we had made while we were at Munro. When I answered the call, it was my father. I have never been able to ascertain how it was that my father was always able to get a hold of my phone number. I don't recall ever giving it to him. Since the last time he had visited me in Florida some nine years before, things had changed between us.

My wife and I were having a discussion one day, and the topic of my parents came up. After listening to me complain about them, she looked and me and said, "You have to forgive your parents if you are going to be able to get on with your life."

"Okay," I responded flippantly, "I forgive them."

"No," she said. "It is going to take more than you casually saying, 'I forgive them.' You are really going to have to do it."

"What do you mean?" I inquired.

"Well, I think you should go and sit down and talk with them and put all this animosity behind you."

"Go?" I said. "Go where?"

"To England," she said. "That is where they live, isn't it?"

She was serious. After giving it some thought, a few months later, my wife and I flew to London to see my parents.

We had arranged to stay at the home of one of the sisters who was born in England. I had first met her when she came with the family to visit. I had also seen her again two years later while I was on a visit to Jamaica. She had always been enthusiastic about her Jamaican brother and was the only one who came all the way from London to be part of my wedding to Scottie. We had grown really fond of her and had kept in frequent contact with her. When I called and told her what I was planning, she quickly volunteered to have us stay with her for our visit. I was happy to accept since at that time, there was no way I wanted to stay in my parents' house.

The day after our arrival in London, I went to see my parents. They were very happy to see us, and they were keen to get to know Scottie who they were meeting for the very first time. My father and I sat down at his dining table and talked for more than six hours that day. It was just us two. My mother was busy doing other things, and Scottie had gone off with my sister. It was during those six hours of conversation that my entire attitude toward my parents changed. I listened as my father relayed story after story about the tremendous difficulties they faced trying to survive in England after they got there. There were times when they were homeless, he said. Since these were just ordinary country people from Jamaica, they knew nothing about birth control, so they just kept having kids until there were six more.

According to my father, it was not that they didn't think about us back in Jamaica, but rather that they were desperately trying just to survive, and that was all they could do. I was so moved by what he was telling me that a sense of shame came over me. I became ashamed for how I had thought of them over all those years and how I had behaved toward them on the few occasions that we had spent together. I had come to England to tell my parents that I forgave them; instead, on that day, I was the one who needed their forgiveness for the rude and disrespectful way I had behaved.

By the time we left London to return to the States, things had changed between my parents and me. It would be wrong to say that we now had a close relationship similar to what I enjoyed with my sons. No, that would probably never happen after all of our past history. But at least now, I knew that the hostility I once harbored toward them for more than forty years was no longer there.

It was during that visit that my dad also shared about another of his regrets, and that was his decision to take one of the daughters born in Jamaica back with him to England in 1973.

Since she was only seventeen years old at the time, she was still considered a minor, and since her father was an English citizen, he could sponsor her to come and live in England. From the time she was growing up in Jamaica, people would often refer to her as "madda peppa" for her fiery personality. The girl was unafraid, and when Dad took her back to England and tried to impose his discipline on her, she was having none of it.

To the shock of her English-born siblings, she would be openly defiant and rude to their parents without any consequences. Before she arrived, the household was run like an army camp with everyone doing as they were told or they would face the wrath of their father.

Our Jamaican-born sister didn't care one bit about her father's wrath, and this allowed the other children to begin to defy him as well without consequences. Her arrival had turned his house upside down.

The funny thing was while her other sisters and brothers were happy to throw off the strict shackles their father had imposed on them, they were also very resentful of her for her rudeness and defiance. But they had no clue about the years of hurts and resentment that had been building up in that girl, and now that she had an opportunity to direct it at the persons she held personally responsible for what she had suffered, she was not holding back.

Maybe it was out of guilt, but Dad felt helpless at the onslaught he was receiving at her hand and slowly watched as the other children literally began to laugh in his face at his futile attempt to reimpose discipline in his house.

And so it was that when I answered the phone that day having returned from Jamaica months earlier and realized that it was my father, my attitude was a lot different.

"Earl," he said, "why did you leave Jamaica, just as I planned to move back?"

"Well, Dad," I said, "I had no idea you were planning to move back to Jamaica."

"Man, I wish you had told me before you moved back to the States."

My father was obviously ignoring what I had just said. I had no idea he had plans to move back to Jamaica from England. He had lived there for nearly fifty years, so why he would choose to move back at that time was beyond me.

As the conversation went on, I began to have a clearer understanding as to why he was sad that I had left Jamaica before he arrived. Apparently, he had chosen to build a house not too far from the school where I had been the principal. As he moved around the community and people realized that he was the father of the former headmaster at Munro, he found that people were a lot more enthusiastic about offering him any help that he needed. And so, he felt that life would have been so much easier for him if I had been there.

"Man, these people here really respected you," he said.

You Need to Go Back to England

I WAS TO have several more conversations with my father while he was living in Jamaica. And with each conversation, I could detect a greater sense of urgency and desperation in his voice. My wife and I had to make at least three or four trips back to Jamaica to look about his welfare.

When my father went back to Jamaica, he was eighty-two years old. The Jamaica he left some fifty years before was nothing like the Jamaica he came back to. His coming back to Jamaica was part of a pattern for Jamaicans who had migrated to the United States, Canada, and England. Having worked hard all their lives and saved their money, many of them returned to the island where they hoped to live the well-to-do lifestyle they couldn't have had if they had stayed in Jamaica. So they would return to the area of the island they were originally from and build themselves big houses to live in as a sign to their old friends that they had made it. However, the quality of life they were used to living in a developed country was not now available to them on the island. At that stage of his life, my father was having some major health issues. Since he couldn't drive and the nearest hospital was at least an hour away, he had to pay someone to drive him to wherever he wanted to go, and they were ripping him off at every chance they got. Soon, he found himself short of cash.

According to my father, he was supposed to be receiving a certain amount of money from England each month, but he was not getting it. When we went to visit him the first time, we found that the house needed some work done to it, the fridge was broken so they couldn't use it, and there was very little food in the house. We did not bring much money with us that would be enough to meet his needs. But we still had a bank account in Jamaica with a substantial amount in it which we withdrew and gave to him. Shortly thereafter, we would be back in Jamaica again to help, and a pattern began to form. Finally, on my last trip, I had seen enough and I told him, "You need to go back home to England."

Jamaica did not have the social security net that countries like the United States and England offer their citizens. With his health issues, my father was finding out that every time he went to see the doctor, he had to pay. This would not have been the case if he had remained in England. In addition, I could see that my mother was beginning to show the early onset of dementia. At this stage of their lives, the quality of life they were going to have if they remained in Jamaica was not going to be good. He agreed, but said he didn't have the funds to purchase tickets back to England. We purchased those tickets too and told them that they really need to get back to England as soon as possible. I was to find out later that upon his arrival back in England, he suffered a heart attack and had to be taken directly to the hospital.

I didn't hear from my father again until about three years later. It was a Sunday afternoon, and we had just finished our church service. I was sitting in my office when my phone rang. It was my father. He told me that he was in the hospital, and no one had come to visit him, so he decided to call me. He said that he was not doing very well and didn't think he had long to live. I thought he was exaggerating and told him that I would make arrangements to fly over to see him that coming weekend.

"I won't be here," he said.

"Ah, come on, Dad," I said. "Surely you can hold on until I get there?"

"I won't be here when you come," he said and hung up.

After sharing the conversation with my wife, we immediately began to make plans to fly to London that coming Saturday. The following day, we were on our way to an appointment when the phone rang. It was my sister.

"Earl," she said. "Dad died last night."

He was eighty-eight years old. I was truly saddened that I didn't get the chance to see him before he died.

I had to spend an entire day at the passport office in Miami, trying to get them to issue me a passport in one day rather than the customary three or four weeks. Apart from the usual paperwork, they also wanted a copy of my dad's death certificate. It meant that I had to have someone call London to get a copy and fax it to the passport office. We arrived in Miami about five in the morning; by the time we got everything sorted out, it was four o'clock in the afternoon.

My wife and I flew to England for the funeral, and while we were there, we took the opportunity to visit with my other brothers and sisters and my mother. I wasn't to see my mother again, and eight years later, we were back in England for her funeral. She died at age ninety-five.

That's Your Daughter?

ONE OF MY favorite family photographs hanging on my wall is the one with my wife, her mother, our oldest daughter, and our first grandchild. It is a picture showing four generations of women. It was taken nearly thirty years ago. It was one of the few pictures we had taken to Jamaica that hung on the wall in the living room of the headmaster's residence.

It was coming to the end of my second year at Munro when I got a phone call from a teacher I knew back in Florida. She taught at the same school I did before I came to Jamaica. She was the chorus teacher, and two of our daughters had been members and leaders of the chorus class, so I knew her well. Every year, she had been able to take her group and trained them to use their vocal abilities to perform to such exceptional levels that the State of Florida consistently rated them "superior." This school year was no different, and as a reward for her kids' outstanding performance, she decided to take them on a special trip to Jamaica. Since she knew I had left Florida to become a principal in Jamaica, she wanted to find out if it would be possible for her to bring them to Munro to see how a Jamaican school operated. I was only too happy to accommodate her.

By this time, my wife's boys' choir had, for the second year in a row, been voted the outstanding gospel choir on the island during the annual independence festival competition. When the choir first began, only boys from the lower school expressed an interest in participating. Many felt that the choir was for sissies, so every Monday morning, during the assembly for the entire school, I would have the boys sing. As they got more and more notoriety for their singing, more and more boys from the upper school wanted to take part. At one point, the choir had grown to over seventy boys. Since the students who were coming to visit were known for their singing, we thought it would be great to have the boys perform for them.

And so, we made all the necessary plans to have these students from Florida come to spend the day at Munro. We would feed them, let them tour the campus, visit several of the classes while they were in session, and finally, we would have the boys sing for them.

I was in the headmaster's residence when the bus carrying the students from Florida arrived. They had been staying in Montego Bay, which was about a three-hour drive from the school. As I finished up what I was doing and rushed down the stairs to go out and meet them, I noticed that one of the ladies from the bus was standing in our living room looking at the picture of our four generations of women on the wall.

"Is that your daughter?" she asked.

"Yes," I said.

"You're Melissa's dad?"

"Yes."

"I didn't know that."

Melissa is our oldest daughter, and the lady in our living room was the wife of the pastor of the church Melissa attended in Florida.

That day could not have gone any better. The students were able to mix with and talk to the boys from Munro, and since most of the visiting students were girls, the boys were only too happy to engage with them.

After the boys' performance, even the teacher who was accustomed to her chorus group being rated superior was impressed. As we were all saying goodbye and the kids were getting on the bus for their drive back to Montego Bay, the pastor's wife came over to me and said, "I would like you to come and preach at my church the next time you are in Florida."

I agreed, and they left.

A Promised Made

AFTER THAT VISIT, I was to spend only another five months in Jamaica before we too left and returned to Florida. We had settled in to a normal routine with me back in the classroom in Florida. About a month after we got back, our daughter Melissa came to visit.

"Pastor wants to know when are you available to come and preach at our church like you promised," she said to me.

"Which church? Which pastor?"

I didn't know what she was talking about. It was then she reminded me that back in Jamaica, the pastor's wife had invited me to come and speak when I was back in Florida and I had said I would.

I hadn't seen the lady since that visit to Munro, so she could only have known that I was back in Florida because Melissa had mentioned it to her. I had totally forgotten about the invitation. In fact, I had not really taken her seriously when she said it to me that day.

During my two-and-a-half-year stay in Jamaica, I had gotten several invitations to speak across the island. I had only been able to accept a few of them, but my reputation as a speaker had become quite well-known. As a result, I had to turn down several invitations to be the guest speaker at different functions.

On one occasion, after I had spoken at a church service that was broadcast live on radio, the radio station contacted me about having my own weekly religious program. When I politely turned it down, the gentleman was shocked and told me that people paid to have their program broadcast on his radio station, and here he was offering me the opportunity at no cost and I was refusing?

"Sorry," I said. "I can't do it."

Even the leading newspaper on the island contacted me about writing a weekly column for their editorial page. That intrigued me since there was so much I wanted to say about my observation of the educational scene in Jamaica, but I had to say no. He then asked if I would consider doing a monthly column for the newspaper. That I could do. I was to get much grief from many people, including some at the Ministry of Education, for the opinions I would express in those monthly columns.

So I had gotten used to people asking me to come and speak and me having to turn them down. And so, eight months before, when the wife of Melissa's pastor spoke to me about coming to her church when I returned to Florida, I had said yes without thinking it would really happen. I had forgotten everything about that conversation. So if our daughter hadn't informed her of my return to Florida, I had no thought of doing so myself.

It was Super Bowl Sunday of 2004 when I went and kept my promise to speak at Melissa's church. After the service, the pastor called my wife and me aside to speak to us.

"I have always had a vision of a one-hundred-voice boys' choir in this area," he said. "Would you two be willing to spearhead such an effort?"

Apparently, after his wife's visit with the students to Jamaica, she had returned and told him about the excellent boys' choir my wife had developed at Munro, and he wanted her to replicate that effort for the local community.

The Avenue D Boys' Choir

Pastor James Brown was his name, and he was one of the best known and most admired pastors throughout the community. He met with us at one of his buildings on Avenue D in Fort Pierce to discuss what we would need to start a boys' choir. We had questions. How would we pay for the needs of the choir? How would we recruit boys for the choir? For every one of our questions, Pastor Brown's response was usually "We'll work it out." He did tell us that we could use his building for rehearsals.

We were about to start something that had never been done before, and we were attempting this in one of the most challenging areas in the city. At the time, the area around Avenue D was best known for drugs and prostitution. Several years before, Mike Wallace, the well-known reporter for *60 Minutes*, had used the very same building we were to use for rehearsal as the backdrop for a piece he did on the drug problems in that area. The building itself was once a juke joint, and you could still smell the foul odor from past activities that still permeated the building as you walked in.

One of the first things we had to decide was what name to give the choir. We decided to name it, The Avenue D Boys' Choir. We chose to name the choir after the avenue because it was our hope that the choir would help to change people's perception of the area.

And so, it was that my wife and I stood outside that notorious building on Avenue D on March 4, 2004, and began recruiting young men for the choir as they walked by. As you can well imagine, we got a lot of dirty looks and some that clearly implied that they thought we were crazy.

After about two weeks, we began our first rehearsal with about ten boys who didn't have a clue about singing. They were all tone-deaf. On top of that, these were problem kids, many of whom had been getting in all sorts of trouble at school and around the community. Maintaining discipline was going to be a challenge. And that was where I came in.

Having been the headmaster of a boys' school, I knew that the presence of a strong black male was going to be paramount if we were going to see changes in the lives of these young men that we were aiming for. One of the very first things I did was to create a mantra for the choir that we had them repeat every time they met for rehearsal. We would have them begin by saying this: "We are young men of honor, pursuing excellence and leading by example."

And we would have them say it twice. After which they would say this:

> I believe!
> I believe I can be a good student and citizen!
> I believe I can achieve great things in my life!
> I believe if I work hard, I will succeed!
> Therefore, I will work hard each day to do my best!
> And I will allow nothing or no one to hinder my success!

In fact, over the fourteen years that the choir existed, those two things were to be repeated at every gathering and every function where the choir performed. It didn't matter if it was just in the local community, along the Treasure Coast of Florida, performing throughout the United States, or touring in Italy and France. It was to become like their second nature where they knew to say it even without any prompting from me or my wife.

Initially, my wife had so much to do that I didn't want her to have to worry about discipline so that became my chief priority. I made sure that I was always a constant presence whether it was at rehearsals or at performances. I wanted the boys to know that

I expected them to learn to act like young men and not like little thugs. One thing I was particularly adamant about was the way they responded and treated my wife. There was not going to be any eye-rolling, shaking of heads, hissing of teeth, or talking back when she spoke to them. They knew that any such action or reaction on their part would guarantee my wrath. At first, it was very challenging, but as time went by, we came to rely on the senior members of the choir to help ensure that the newer members toed the line. Many of them took it as their personal responsibility to make sure that my wife was always protected.

When we first started the choir, we had no source from which we could get funds, so all the cost came out of our pockets. One thing that we quickly realized, especially at the beginning stage of the choir, was that if we wanted the boys to keep coming back, we had to feed them. And that is what we did. For the fourteen years the choir was in existence, we would always make sure they were fed after every rehearsal and after every performance. For many of these boys, this meal was all they would have had to eat that day.

As the choir began to grow, we knew that we had to find some funding, and that was when we found out about Children Service Council of Port St. Lucie. This was an organization especially set up by the state to help provide funds to organizations that were affecting the lives of people, particularly young people, in a positive way. When we approached them and shared what we wanted to do, they told us they couldn't fund us because we were only going to let the boys sing gospel songs. We told them that teaching them gospel was part of the plan to help change their lives. They wanted us to include other secular songs in what they did, and we told them we couldn't do that. Several days later, we got a call from the director telling us that they had found a way to provide funds for the choir even though they were still only going to be singing gospel. And so, for the entire life of the choir, the one consistent and main source of income for the choir was the Children Services Council of St. Lucie County.

Spreading Their Wings

As WORD GOT around the community that there was a boys' choir from the area that could really sing, it wasn't long before the invitations for the boys to come and perform started rolling in. These were some very talented boys. Most of them might have been tone-deaf when we began, but they were far from that now. And it wasn't just singing that the boys did. My wife also began putting choreography to their singing so that when they performed, it was a show, not just singing. My wife had seen the importance of adding movement to singing when she was at Munro. The first year she entered the choir in the national festival in Jamaica, they were the only ones doing any movement to their singing; by the second year, every choir in the finals was doing movement. Since the boys were becoming more and more enthused with their singing, having them incorporate movement became a breeze.

We were in rehearsal with the boys one day when we got a visit from a local businessman. He was a personal friend of a well-known Grammy Award–winning R&B singer from the 1970s. Joe Simon was best known for his R&B hits "Choking Kind" and "Letter to Maria." Over the years, he had disappeared from the secular music scene and was now a bishop going around the country preaching and singing. He was coming to Fort Pierce and wanted to get a community choir he could use to provide backup vocals to his singing. The businessman told him about us, and so it was that the boys sang with Joe Simon the night he came to Fort Pierce. He was so impressed that he asked my wife if they could accompany him to his next venue which was in St. Augustine, Florida, which they did.

About a week later, we got a call from Joe Simon himself advising that he had been invited to sing some gospel songs at a festival in Italy and would love to have the boys come with him to provide the backup vocals he would need. We readily agreed, and he sent us a list of ten songs with the specific instruction that the boys had to learn all the songs, not just the chorus. Joe Simon lived in Chicago, and we were in Florida. We knew right away that there was not going to be any chance for the boys to rehearse with him. But why did he want the boys to know all the songs by heart? I wondered. We were to find out later.

The trip to Italy was four months away, and we had no funds. In addition, not a single boy had ever traveled out of the country. In fact, only a few of them had even been out of Florida. It meant that we had to get passports for them; it meant uniforms. There was going to be a whole array of things that were needed before we could possibly hope to get to Italy.

Thank God for Debbie Riggs. Debbie was one of our volunteers and was a wiz at planning and logistics. So while she went about making all the arrangements for the boys to get to Italy and for their stay there, my wife went about raising the funds we would need to get everything done. In four months, she was able to raise nearly one hundred thousand dollars for the trip. Debbie was also able to fit the boys into a stopover in Paris on our way home from Italy.

Joe Simon had been invited to sing at a festival being held in a little Italian town named Porretta Terme. The festival was held each year as a tribute to the American soul singer Otis Redding who had died in the late 1960s at the very height of his fame. Redding is better remembered for such songs as "Dock of the Bay," "Try a Little Tenderness," and "I've Got Dreams to Remember." The festival was going to be from July 17 to 20, 2008, and featured a slew of renowned secular artiste like Chaka Khan, Sugar Pie DeSanto, Mable John, Henry Butler, and Otis Redding III among many others. Joe Simon was the only artist performing gospel.

For years, promoters had been trying to get him to return to performing his old secular hits, but he refused. After he became a Christian, he pledged himself to only singing gospel songs. The only reason the promoters of the Porretta Terme Festival were able to get him to come was because they assured him that he would only be required to sing gospel songs.

The news of the boys' trip to Europe quickly spread along the Treasure Coast, and they were asked to appear on local television and on local radio stations talking about the upcoming trip. A week before the festival was to start, the choir of twenty-five boys and twenty-five chaperones flew out of Miami to Paris and then on to Italy. When we arrived in Paris, we had to wait for nearly four hours for repairs to be done to the plane taking us to Italy. We arrived in Italy late in the afternoon, got on the bus that was waiting for us, and headed to the hotel. The whole group was so tired by then that we all went to bed and crashed.

There was no doubt about the excitement that was generated in that little Italian town when the boys went out to walk around the following day. Everywhere they went, people followed them. The night Joe Simon and the boys were to perform, there was a sound check early that afternoon, and the amphitheater was packed. The night of the performance, there were so many people there that my wife had to stand in the crowd as she attempted to conduct the choir as they accompanied Joe Simon through his ten songs. It was that night that it became clear why Joe had wanted the boys to learn all the songs by heart. As he sung, we noticed that he would often forget the words, but it didn't matter because the boys would just keep right on singing so he could catch up.

After the festival, we left Italy and flew into Paris early in the afternoon and decided to take the boys for a walk around the city. We ended up in front of Notre Dame Cathedral, and standing in front of its huge front door, the boys began to sing a cappella. A crowd soon gathered and began following the boys as we walked around. I became concerned that there might be a problem, and so I went back in the crowd and asked a gentleman why he was following us.

"Because we want to hear them sing again," he said.

The following day, the boys did an impromptu concert at the hotel where we were staying, and all the guests gathered on the balconies in front of their rooms to listen and applaud the boys for their performance. After three days in Paris, we flew back to America. The boys had had an experience they would not soon forget, and the fame of the Avenue D Boys' Choir continued to grow.

The Avenue D Boys' Choir would become so well-known and popular that they were booked months in advance to be the entertainment for several country clubs' annual Christmas parties.

I Have No Such Interest

FROM THE TIME I was a teenager teaching Sunday school, I had been told that I had a gift for ministry. I didn't believe it nor did I want to be a minister. One of my best friends had gone off to seminary to study to be a pastor in the Methodist Church, but I had no interest in joining him there. Instead, I went off to teachers' college. But I did continue to teach and preach in churches and at church events.

In 2001, just before we left for Jamaica, the pastor of the church we attended approached me about being ordained a minister in the church. I agreed. So when I went to Jamaica, I went as an ordained minister of the gospel as well. When I returned to Florida and spoke at Pastor Brown's church, it wasn't long before he approached me about becoming the pastor of a satellite church he wanted to start. I was not interested, and so he began working on my wife. She relayed this conversation they had.

"Does your husband know that the Lord has called him to be a pastor?"

"Yes," she said, "but he's running from it."

But Pastor Brown persisted, and finally, I said yes.

He wanted to start the church in the very same building on Avenue D that we were using for choir rehearsal. At the time, I was leading a Bible study in a friend's house that consisted of about twenty people. I told them of the plan to start the new church, and they all agreed that they would be part of it. After the first new members' orientation, fourteen of the people—all white—left without saying a word to me. Even the lady whom I had asked to be my associate pastor left without an explanation. It meant that when the new church started, there were only eight of us.

Apart from the building and the chairs, Pastor Brown and the main church provided us with no other support. In fact, we had to pay the mortgage on the building, the light bill, and do all the repairs using only the funds collected from the seven people. Pastor Brown had made sure to open a bank account for the church with his and my names on the account. It was not something that I thought of as being significant at the time, but I was to find out that it was.

Along with doing the choir, my wife and I were now pastors. I was also a vice principal at one of the local high schools. The church grew in numbers, and within eighteen months, we had membership of about twenty-seven people. Most of our new members were boys who were members of the choir and other family members. The one thing I noticed was that we could not get white folks to come to the church. We had one older white couple who had been with us from the beginning, and that was it. It was then that I began to realize that the location of the church had a lot to do with it. Avenue D was right in the middle of a black neighborhood. It was once the most notorious avenue in the entire town, and most outsiders just weren't comfortable coming there. I realized that if the church was going to grow, we needed to move its location. The problem was Pastor Brown had been adamant that that was where the new church should be. I was left wondering how I was going to get him to change his mind. As it turned out, I didn't change his mind, he changed mine.

Time for a Change

ONE OF THE reasons I had been willing to accept being a pastor was the way I saw Pastor Brown conducted himself. He was warm and friendly and had a genuine concern for people. He would walk along Avenue D and greet each person passing by, engaged them in conversation, and would often say a prayer for them before saying goodbye. I admired him for that. But about eighteen months after we started the church on Avenue D, I began to detect some subtle changes being directed at us from the main church. I couldn't exactly put my finger on the reason for the change in attitude, but I surmised that it could have had something to do with the fact that we were not having Pastor Brown or any of the leaders from his church to come and speak at our Sunday morning services. My reason for that was simple. At Pastor Brown's church, they screamed when they preached, and the louder, the better. That wasn't for me. I just did not believe in screamers. These were preachers who hooped and hollered and screamed into the microphone as loud as they could. I felt that people were more likely to grow spiritually if there was more teaching of the Word of God than what I called screaming preaching.

My position on the matter was further confirmed when we took the boys to sing at a Spanish-speaking church. As I stood up to introduce the boys, I noticed that there were some writings, in Spanish of course, on the wall at the back of the church. Because the writing was in the direct sight of whosoever was on the platform, I thought that it was probably there for the speakers than for the regular congregant.

And so, after the performance, I asked the pastor what the writing said. He said, "Please don't push my people." Seeing the puzzled look on my face, he went on to explain.

Among most charismatic churches, being slain in the Spirit is a normal part of worship. It is when someone is so moved by the Spirit of God that they fall to the ground. It seemed that preachers who had preached at this pastor's church had been helping people to the ground by pushing them. The pastor felt that this was wrong, and so he put up a sign in large letters on the wall in the direct view of any preacher, not to push his people when they prayed for them.

Obviously, this pastor was not comfortable having visiting speakers pushing his people, and he wanted them to know. If someone is comfortable and happy going to a church where they scream and holler, that is fine. It just wasn't my preference, and therefore, I would rather not have it in our church.

And so, eighteen months after the church began, the main church suddenly requested that we return two little containers they had given to us to use for receiving the offering on Sunday mornings. I thought that was a strange request, but we did send back their two little containers.

Soon after that, the main church celebrated its twenty-fifth anniversary with a banquet at the club house of a local country club. We were invited, and when we arrived, we found that they had seated my wife and me at the back of the room near the bathroom. At the head table were many local politicians, and during the night's festivities and speech making, not once did they acknowledge the Avenue D church. It was as if we didn't exist. The following day, I received word that Pastor Brown wanted me to close down our service for the coming Sunday morning, and we were all to come to the main church for service instead. I sent back word that we couldn't do that since we didn't have a chance to announce it to our people. We didn't want people turning up for service, only to find the doors locked with no explanation. We were particularly sensitive to this since we were beginning to have visitors, and I didn't want someone who was invited to come and we were not there. I did offer to start our service two hours earlier so that those who wanted to could go on to the main church for the service there. And that is what we did.

During the service at the main church, the leadership of the church proceeded to crown Pastor Brown and his wife with crowns and sashes made up of one-hundred-dollar bills, and they then sashayed back and forth across the platform, waving like they were a king and a queen. Right then and there, I realized what I had to do.

I had wanted to talk to Pastor Brown about moving the location of the church and so I called and make an appointment to speak with him. I made certain that only my wife accompanied me to the meeting. I began by telling him about my concerns about the location of the church having a negative impact on the growth of the church.

"Location has nothing to do with the growth of a church" was his response. It was then that it seemed as if he suddenly realized something. "Are you planning on leaving from under the main church?" he asked.

"Yes, sir, I am."

I really had not planned on telling him that. I was considering it but had not yet made up my mind. But when he asked the question, I answered in the affirmative without thinking.

"Let me tell you a story," he said. Whereupon he proceeded to tell me a story about a spider that had grown fat from all the food he was able to catch in his web. But one day, he looked at the spawn hanging from the ceiling and asked, "What have you done for me lately?"

The spider then proceeded to cut down the spawn, and his entire web went crashing to the ground.

I don't know if he was trying to scare me or what, but I didn't see how that story related to me. I had not grown fat from anything that he or his church had provided to me. The church on Avenue D was self-sustaining, and I was not even taking a salary from what was taken for collection. If anything, we were the ones who had conferred a benefit on to him by paying the mortgage on the building on Avenue D. He had also insisted that our tithe, which was substantial, should be sent to his church. When I told him that I think our tithe should be coming to our church, he was adamant that his church should receive it and not ours, so I complied. His church had never given us a dime in the eighteen months we were there. When I left him that Tuesday night, I was very sad in my spirit because I had begun to see a side of him that was not what I had expected. But more was still to come.

It All Belongs to Me

When my wife and I left our meeting with Pastor Brown that Tuesday night, we had no idea what we were going to do going forward. Like I said, I hadn't planned on telling him that we were separating from him and his church, so we had no plan in place to accommodate that. During that week, I tried to contact as many of our members as possible to let them know about the meeting and what had happened.

The following Sunday morning, we all gathered for service as usual. I was not the speaker that day, so I sat up front as I usually do. As the service progressed, I became aware that Pastor Brown was in the audience. I was a little surprised to see him. In the eighteen months the church had been in operation, he had probably visited us about three times. I didn't pay much attention to him until when the service was drawing to a close, I noticed that he had moved from the rear and was sitting immediately behind me. When the speaker had finished and before we could dismiss the members, Pastor Brown got up and said he wanted to say something. I told him fine. He proceeded to tell the congregation about our conversation, and after expressing his disappointment, he told them that all the money in the bank account was his. That if we chose to move from under his auspices, we couldn't have it. I was shocked. You could hear the audible gasps from the members.

By this time, some members had started to cry. I had heard enough. I got up and dismissed the service and ask that only the leadership stay behind so we could talk with Pastor Brown. When everyone had left the building, I turned to Pastor Brown and told him that if he had told me at our meeting on Tuesday that he wanted the money in the account, I would gladly have let him have it. For him to come to the church to announce to our members what he just did was unnecessary. Besides, I told him, I had not taken a salary in the eighteen months the church had been in operation, so maybe I should be paid with some of that money.

"Oh no," he said. "It isn't my fault you chose not to take at salary."

At the time, there was nearly twenty thousand dollars in the bank account. Since his name was on the account, he usually got a copy of each monthly statement from the bank. So when he came that Sunday morning, he knew exactly how much was in the account. I was getting more and more disgusted. When several of our leaders began expressing disappointment with what he had done, he finally got up, threw up his arms, and as he walked out, he said, "Do whatever you want with it."

We immediately decided that we would form a new church and transfer the moneys to that church's account. And that was when Family of Faith Worship Center was born.

Pastor Brown wasn't finished. When the choir first began, the need for a van to transport the boys became apparent. Pastor Brown provided the initial down payment for us to get the van, but the monthly payments became our responsibility. He took back the van. He also informed us that since the boys' choir was his idea, he was taking that too. This was just about three years after the choir started and was quickly gaining much notoriety along the Treasure Coast of Florida. But this was easier said than done.

The choir had grown to over fifty boys who had developed a very close relationship with my wife. They were very loyal to her and weren't going to be going off with whomsoever Pastor Brown thought he could get to run the choir. He quickly gave up on that idea. And so, in quick succession, we didn't have a building for the new church to meet, and the boys' choir now had nowhere to rehearse.

Searching for a Place

My wife and I got busy trying to find some vacant building that we could use for our church services as well as for the choir rehearsals. Since the choir met three times a week for rehearsal, finding a place for them was the most urgent. We went all around the town of Fort Pierce looking for a place. Finally, someone suggested that we could use one of the classrooms at an elementary school. It was a very small room, but we used it until a local church called and offered us their fellowship hall. We gladly accepted the offer, but had to leave after about four weeks because the pastor reneged on his promise that we could use the space free of charge. One day, he came and informed us that we would have to start paying rent. He never explained why he changed his mind about us using the place for free.

We finally ended finding a more appropriate place for our rehearsals when the Methodist Church in downtown Fort Pierce called to offer their fellow hall for our use. In the two years we were there, they didn't charge us a dime. In fact, they would often make financial contributions to help with the cost of running the choir.

Finding a place for the new church was more challenging. The one thing we were certain of was that we did not want to keep the church on Avenue D. One afternoon, as I was driving west on Avenue D coming from US 1, for some reason, I began to count how many churches there were on Avenue D. From Seventh Street to Twentieth Street and Avenue D where our church was located, I counted fourteen different churches. That was virtual one church per block. No, we would have to get as far away from that area as possible. We had a week to find a place.

I don't recall how we heard, but word got to us that there was a fellowship in Jensen Beach, which was about an hour's drive from Fort Pierce that was moving from their building to a larger space nearby. We contacted the pastor, and he invited us down to speak with him and his leadership team. After our meeting, they agreed to rent us the building. It meant that every Thursday night for Bible study and every Sunday morning for worship service, my wife and I, along with the majority of the nearly twenty-seven members, drove the hour down to Jensen Beach to meet.

The building was in a predominantly white neighborhood, and during our time there, we were not able to engage with anyone in the immediate surroundings because we lived so far away. We did not add a single new member while we were meeting in Jensen Beach, and the few visitors we did have were usually family members of those already attending.

We were there from March until September when the pastor told us that they were going to need their building back by the end of the month. Apparently, their plans to purchase an old grocery store to turn into their new place of worship had fallen through, and they decided to renovate their old building instead.

So after only six months, our new church was homeless again. It was during that time that some of my spiritual uncertainties began to surface again. This wasn't what I had signed up for, and I was beginning to wonder if this was really what I wanted to be doing after all.

Wasted Years

I WAS ABOUT fifteen years old when I first became conscious of the fact that I was a sinner in need of a Savior. And so, one summer night at a Bible camp in Jamaica, I gave my heart to the Lord. And I wish I could say that my life after that night became one beautiful example of godliness and Christlikeness. It didn't; it wasn't. In fact, for the next nearly thirty years of my life, I struggled with this faith I said I had embraced.

It just seemed that no matter how hard I tried, I could never measure up. I also had a terrible temper, and it wouldn't take much to set me off. And every time I would lose my temper, I would get very disgusted with myself, and I would start all over again, asking for forgiveness and promising to try harder next time.

I was in my forties before I even came to understand that the God of the Bible really did love me. Not because of what I had done or because of how pleased he was with me, but that he loved me just because he chose to do so. That was a revelation to me! Now mark you, during all those years, I had developed a reputation as a preacher and teacher and had been invited to several churches and gospel meetings to preach and teach. And while I was busy teaching and preaching about this love of God, it was not something that I was experiencing for myself.

In 2001, I was ordained a minister of the gospel and continued to preach and teach, albeit by now, I had a little better understanding of God's love for me. But I was still struggling with doubts about my own salvation. I even began doubting my call to be a pastor because I just could not see how I measured up. I was constantly trying to live up to the standards I thought God wanted me to live up to, and the more I examined myself, the more I would see how far short I kept falling.

During all this time, a lot of my preaching and teaching focused on living a godly life in this world—one that no matter how hard I was trying, I always felt that I was never quite there.

And if you had known me back then, you would probably have thought that I was a very godly man. I wasn't doing any of the things that people thought of as being worldly. Growing up in the '60s and '70s, I didn't do drugs or drink or run around. On the outside, I seemed to be the epitome of a godly man who knew what he was about. And yet inside, I was constantly at war with myself.

I knew the Bible said that God loved me, but was I proving myself worthy of that love? And besides, why, why should he love me anyway? My parents had abandoned me at age five, and I grew up with an English family. And even though I could see how much they cared for me, I was always suspicious as to whether I, a little black boy, could ever be fully accepted into a white family where they already had seven children of their own.

Soon after I became an adult, my adopted parents upped and died on me. And I was left wondering yet again that if the people who were supposed to love me kept leaving me, then God certainly had absolutely no reason to love me. I had done nothing to deserve his love, so why?

In 2005, some forty years after I first gave my life to the Lord, my wife and I started Family of Faith Worship Center in Fort Pierce. I was fifty-four years old at the time and now had to begin to read and study the Bible in earnest in order to be prepared to preach and teach each Sunday morning. It was about two years after we started the fellowship that, glory to God, the Lord began to open my eyes to his amazing grace.

Now, I know that might sound a little strange to some people. How is it possible to have been preaching and teaching all those years and still had so little or no understanding of the grace of God? Very easy, really!

Like a lot of people, I grew up in churches where the predominant message was about hell and brimstone. It was mainly about the judgment of God. It was about what I should or should not be doing as a Christian. The gist of the message was basically, if you wanted God's blessings, you gotta do this and you gotta do that or else! And I took those things really seriously.

So I spent all those years trying to prove to God that I was worthy, but I never came to a time or place where I felt that yes, I had proven myself worthy, that I had earned his love. I grew up thinking that God was a god who was easily offended by every little thing I did wrong or the things I failed to do.

Looking back now, I realize that what I had heard growing up and what I ended up preaching was a mixture of God's grace and my own best efforts: God loves you and saves you, but you had better make sure that your life shows that you deserved that love.

Liberated by Grace

As I BEGAN to look seriously into scripture, I discovered passages like Roman 8:1–4, "So there is therefore now, no condemnation for those who belong to Christ Jesus. And because you belong to him, the power of the life-giving Spirit has freed you from the power of sin that leads to death. The Law of Moses was unable to save us because of the weakness of our sinful nature. So, God did what the law could not do. He sent his own Son in a body like the bodies we sinners have. And in that body God declared an end to sin's control over us by giving his Son as a sacrifice for our sins. He did this so that the just requirement of the law would be fully satisfied for us, who no longer follow our sinful nature but instead follow the Spirit."

Now, it is one thing to know something intellectually, but it is quite another to know that thing in your heart and in your spirit. I knew a lot of things intellectually, but had a very limited grasp of those things spiritually. If someone had asked me back then, I would have told them that grace meant God's unearned and unmerited favor. I knew that in my intellect, but somehow, I had never been able to transfer that truth to my spirit or accept it as meaning me.

Revelation came to me when I finally realized that I could not earn, I could not work hard enough or long enough to be considered worthy of anything from God. As long I as continued to strive and work hard to show how faithful I was being, the more I realized what a poor, wretched sinner I was. Always trying, but never quite getting there. This was very frustrating and miserable, and that was what I was!

And so, I spent that greater part of my adult life as a Christian being miserable and undone, because I was always conscious of how far short I kept falling, trying hard to prove that I was worthy of God's love and righteousness when I wasn't and I couldn't be!

That was what I realized when I read Galatians 5:4–6, "For if you are trying to make yourselves right with God by keeping the law, you have been cut off from Christ! You have fallen away from God's grace. But we who live by the Spirit eagerly wait to receive by faith the righteousness God has promised to us. For when we place our faith in Christ Jesus, there is no benefit in being circumcised or being uncircumcised." What is important is faith expressing itself in love.

One passage of scripture in particular that has really cleared up this matter of grace and grace alone for me is Luke chapter 9. The Bible says that "as he was praying, the appearance of his face was transformed, and his clothes became dazzling white" (Luke 9:29 NLT).

Then two of the most illustrious figures in the Old Testament and the Jewish faith, Moses and Elijah, appeared and began speaking with Jesus.

> And Peter, feeling that he had to say something but not quite knowing exactly what it is he should say, blurted out: "Master, it is good for us to be here; and let us make three tabernacles: one for You, one for Moses, and one for Elijah."

Now, on the face of it, there does not seem to be anything particularly wrong with what he said. After all, Moses and Elijah were both godly men. They had walked with the Lord, had spoken with him, and had done great things in the name of the Lord. But what Peter did not realize was that, by saying what he said, he was putting Jesus on the same level as Moses and Elijah. And notice that immediately after he did that, God the Father spoke from heaven to correct him.

> While Peter was still speaking, a voice came out of the cloud and said, "This is My beloved Son. Hear Him!" When the disciples heard that, they fell

faced down to the ground, terrified. And then the Lord Jesus came over to them, touched them and said, "Arise, and do not be afraid" (Matthew 17:7).

When they looked up, they saw no one except the Lord Jesus and him alone! When the Lord Jesus comes over to them, touched them in gentle assurance and warmth, and said, "Arise, and do not be afraid," that was a beautiful expression of his amazing grace! His first words when his disciples were terrified were not words of condemnation or words of laws and commandments. No! They were words of grace. And in those words, we can clearly see the very heart and nature of our Savior, "Arise, and do not be afraid." His presence and his words are always designed to lift us up never to tear us <u>down</u>.

But the part of this story that really caught my attention was what God the Father said: "This is my beloved Son. Hear him!"

Notice that he did not say, "Hear them." He said, "Hear him."

On that mount of our Lord's transfiguration, Moses and Elijah were standing right there together with Jesus. Moses was the lawgiver and Elijah was not just an Old Testament prophet, but he was also the law-restorer.

But now, here was God himself making it very clear that the Law and the prophets were not as important as his Son. If we don't hear anything or anyone else, we are to make sure to hear his Son!

For us believers, the Law of Moses has served its purpose which was to bring man to the end of himself. The prophets have also served their purpose of reminding man of God's laws. Both had served their purposes.

But now today, today, is the day of grace. It is the day of the Son of God, not of the servants of God, not of Moses and Elijah, but of the Son of God himself—Jesus Christ, the Savior of the World!

In Acts 4:12, it reads, "Nor is there salvation in any other, for there is no other name under heaven given among men by which we must be saved."

The unfortunate thing that I have observed is that there are still far too many preachers and believers today who want to put Jesus and grace on the same level as the Law of Moses, on the same level as Moses and Elijah!

It became very clear to me that the Law of Moses was not the means by which we are made righteous. By the Law is not the knowledge of the holiness and the righteousness of God, but by the Law is the knowledge of sin! The only thing that the Law can do is show us how sinful we are, how wretched we are, and how much we are in need of a savior.

Paul addressed this for me in Romans 3:20–22, "Therefore by the deeds of the law no flesh will be justified in His sight, for by the law is the knowledge of sin. But now the righteousness of God apart from the law is revealed, being witnessed by the Law and the prophets, [who witnessed it but Moses and Elijah] even the righteousness of God, through faith in Jesus Christ, to all and on all who believe."

But now! It is the "now" revelation of the righteousness of God given to us as a gift apart from the law and this revelation comes through the Son, so hear him!

This is why Moses (the Law) and Elijah (the Prophets) were both witnesses to how we are to "Hear him," the Son and his grace alone for that is what will lift us up today out of any life of sin and misery that we face, so hear him!

It was Jesus who said, "I am the way, the Truth and the Life. No one comes to the Father except through me!" (John 14:6).

And so, I stopped spending my time struggling and wondering if I would ever measure up, if I would ever be good enough, if I would ever be worthy enough.

It became abundantly clear to me that you can only be made righteous and you are made righteous when you trust the finished work of the Lord Jesus Christ for you on the cross. He alone is our righteousness.

And so, while today I am eternally grateful and can boast in the liberating grace of God for me and to me, that I was not how I felt that September day when we found ourselves with nowhere for our church to meet again.

A New Search Begins

ONCE AGAIN, WE began our desperate search to find a place for our church. We must have checked just about everywhere we could and found nothing that was suitable. Finally, we saw an open bay in a strip mall along US 1. The owner said she would be willing to rent us the space, but she had promised it to someone else and would have to wait to hear if they were going to take the space or not. So while we waited to hear from her, we continued our search.

One of our early volunteers with the choir was a young lady whose mother had helped us find our house to buy after we came back from Jamaica. She had originally worked as a nurse, but had switched professions and had gone into real estate. Since her daughter volunteered with the choir, she would often come to the boys' performances. It must have been on one of those occasions that my wife discussed with her about us looking for a place for our church.

One day, she called my wife and told her an interesting story. She said that as she was leaving the Realty Association building in Stuart, she was approached by a gentleman asking about a church that held services in the building. She assured him that no church services were held in that building. When the gentleman insisted that it was so, she went back inside and asked the secretary if a church did, in fact, meet in the building. The secretary told her yes. It was then that she remembered that there was also a Realty Association in Port St. Lucie and they had an auditorium. Maybe, she suggested, we could go and find out if they would rent us the space for our church to meet.

When we met the manager of the Realty Association of Port St. Lucie, she was only too happy to rent the space to us. She had heard of the work we were doing with the boys' choir, had attended some of their performances, and said that they would be more than happy to have us as tenants.

The amount they were charging us for rent was substantially less than what the owner of that open bay on US 1 said she would charge. Apart from the building, they also allowed us to use their sound system as well. So we were very happy with the arrangements we had with them, and we stayed there for just over three years before we moved again, but this time, it was to be into our own building.

As for that space in the strip mall on US 1, we never did hear back from the owner, but we did notice that it was nearly a year later before anyone moved into that empty bay.

A Place with Space

WE BEGAN TO save very aggressively toward purchasing a building of our own. We knew that it was not going to be easy, and so we made sure that we spent money only on the bare essentials. As the pastor, I refused to take any salary since I was still working as an educator in the school system. And while we waited to save enough money, a number of interesting things happened that would affect both the choir and the church going forward.

One day, as we were traveling through town, we noticed a newly erected For Sale sign outside a church building in Fort Pierce. The church was a predominantly white church that had been losing members over the years, and they had decided to sell the building and move on. Part of the reason, I supposed, was that the demographics of the area was changing, and the white members were no longer comfortable traveling to a predominantly black area for church services.

The location of the building was perfect. It was right at the intersection of two busy roads, which meant that it was easily seen and accessible. But when we checked with the realtor, the price they were asking for the building was way too much for us, so we weren't able to purchase it.

Just about that same time we were contacted by a businessman who owned properties in Fort Pierce. He had a building downtown and the ground floor was empty and he wanted to know if we could use the space. We went to see it and were thrilled with what we saw.

Not only did it have a lot of open space that could accommodate the boys for rehearsals, it also had two offices and lots of storage space.

At this juncture of the choir, we had been accumulating a lot of stuff for the choir with nowhere to store them. Things like musical instruments as well as uniforms for the more than fifty boys. The office space would allow us to have a place for meetings and to store documents, some of them legal documents, for the choir. The additional space also allowed us to be able to expand the tutoring services that we were now offering to those boys who needed help with their schoolwork.

Doing well in school was vital if they wanted to continue singing with the choir. To that end, we got the permission of their parents for us to get copies of their nine weeks' reports so we could more closely monitor their grades. In the fourteen years the choir existed, not a single boy who came to the choir and stayed with the choir failed to graduate from high school.

More than three hundred boys were to come through the choir in the fourteen years of its existence. Some stayed only for a while, but every single boy who stayed graduated high school. Several of our boys also went on to college. One was awarded the Bill and Melinda Gates Scholarship to study at Morehouse College in Georgia. We were also able to establish a scholarship fund to help those who chose to remain in the area and attend the local community college.

That space downtown also allowed us to put up a marquee with the name of the choir with its mantra clearly printed out in big bold letters above the entrance. It meant that it was now easier for people to know who we were and where to find us.

When the Impossible Almost Happened

As THE BOYS continued to perform around the community, it gave us the opportunity to meet folks that we would probably not have come in contact with. One such person was Pastor James Biles. Pastor Biles pastored a predominantly white church in the northern part of Fort Pierce. He had invited the boys on several occasions to sing at his church. My wife and I had also developed a close relationship with him, and every Tuesday, we would go and sit and talk and pray with him. Early one morning, I was in my office downtown when I was told that Pastor Biles was there to see me. I was very happy to see him and invited him into my office so we could talk.

Pastor Biles had come to me with the most revolutionary idea. Since he was getting up in age, he had been giving serious thought to retiring soon. He had an idea that he wanted to run by me to see if I would agree with it. He told me that he had been thinking that it would be an excellent idea if we were to combine both churches, that he would remain the senior pastor for one year, after which he would then retire and I would take over.

I was shocked at the suggestion. I had never heard of a white church that wanted to join forces with a black church before. I was intrigued by the idea. I also thought that it would send a very powerful message throughout the community if we were able to do what he was suggesting. I told him that I was very much interested in the idea, and after talking some more, we parted with a promise to have the leadership of both churches meet to hash out the details. We also thought that this was something that we definitely should discuss with our membership as well.

About a week later, we met for our first meeting. I had my wife and our two associate pastors with me. Pastor Biles had about six people with him. Only one member of our team was white, all of his were. As we got down to talking, I noticed that we were being asked a lot of questions about how we collected money at our church. Apparently, someone had gotten one of our offering envelopes that showed the different ways, such as Sunday school, missions, and tithes, that people could give to the church. They wanted to know if people were required to give to all the different areas every Sunday. All their questions seemed to be focusing on our practices in the church; none of it had anything to do with what we might have in common or what we believed.

Since nothing was resolved after that first meeting, we decided to meet again the following week.

At the second meeting, they began again with questions about our practices, and I began to realize that something was amiss here. So I asked them to spell out specifically what concerns they were having with the way we did church. They tried to assure us that all they were seeking were clarifications so that there wouldn't be any misunderstandings between us going forward. But I suspected that there was more to it than they were saying. And because we still were unable to come to any concrete decisions, we ended the meeting, and Pastor Biles told me he would be in touch.

About three days later, I received a letter from Pastor Biles, and in it, he laid out his proposal for the combining of the churches. Among his proposals was that we should go ahead and combine both fellowships, and if after one year, things were not going the way we thought they should, then we would split up and go our separate ways. There was nothing in his letter about him serving for only one year before turning the church over to me. I read and reread the letter several times before I wrote my response.

I began by telling him that the idea of combining the church for one year to see if it worked was a nonstarter for me. I pointed out that during that year, all the tithes and offerings from the members of my church would be going to his church, and if after a year, things weren't working out and they split from us, we would be left with nothing to show for the year we were with him.

I told him that not only was that totally unacceptable to me, but that I had concluded that it was best that we moved on and forget about any idea of combining the churches.

It had become clear to me that the white members of his congregation were not going to be comfortable having a black man as their pastor. It meant that even if I were to become the pastor, I would be totally at their mercy. Nothing was going to be in the name of our church, and it was very possible that after Pastor Biles left that they could simply decide that they didn't want me there and there was nothing I would have been able to do about it. I told Pastor Biles that, in the words of a poker term, "I am out."

The next time I saw Pastor Biles, he expressed to me how unhappy he was at the tone of my letter. He felt that I came across in my letter as being angry and strident, and he demanded that I apologize. I told him there was nothing for me to apologize for since I wasn't angry when I wrote the letter, I was only responding to his letter. That was the last time I was to see or speak to Pastor Biles, and the grand vision he had of combining a black church with a white church was not to materialize.

A Home of Our Own

It was the afternoon of my last meeting with Pastor Biles that my wife and I were driving past the same church building that had been up for sale the year before. Apparently, no one had bought it and they had taken the sign down. But now, here it was, back up again. I told my wife to call the realtor again to find out about it. She was reluctant to do since we had made inquiry the year before only to find out that the price was way out of our range.

"Call again," I insisted. She did, and the realtor offered to meet us at the building to do a walkthrough and see it for ourselves.

The following day, we met the real estate agent at the building, and she took us through and showed us all the space that was available. They were selling the building with everything in it except the sound system. It meant that there would be over two hundred chairs and some tables in excellent condition that we wouldn't have to buy if we bought the building.

When we asked what price they were asking for the building, she told us one that was over a hundred thousand dollars less than they were asking the year before. We were thrilled. It was then that she told us that she was a part of the leadership at the church and had felt all along that we were the ones to whom they should sell the building.

When we first checked into purchasing the building the year before, we had also begun contacting banks to find out if we could secure a mortgage. We found out that banks were not offering mortgages on church buildings. There was one bank though that told us that they would consider our application. A week later, the bank sent us a letter saying that they were no longer doing business in our area. They were being bought out by a larger bank.

No sooner had we gone back and looked at the building again that we received a phone call from the vice president of one of the banks asking that we come in to see her. She had been a vice president at the bank that was taken over and had retained the same position with the new bank. Now that things had settled down, she remembered our application and called to find out if we were still interested in getting a mortgage for the church building. We told her we were and went to see her to discuss the details. Since our church had no financial history to speak of, the bank was only willing to give us a mortgage if my wife and I agreed to be the ones personally responsible for paying the mortgage. We had no problem agreeing to that stipulation.

Despite the more attractive price for the building, we were still some thirty thousand dollars short of the amount that we would need for the down payment. We had no idea where we were going to get that amount of money. In the six-year history of the church from when we first started on Avenue D up to that moment, we had been able to save close to eighty thousand dollars. For down payment and other closing cost, we needed to have about a hundred and ten thousand dollars.

It was on one of her regular visits to see her mother that my wife mentioned our need.

"Baby," she said, "I can lend you that amount."

My wife was shocked. "Mom, where do you have that kind of money?"

"Don't you worry about it" was her simple response.

And so, it was that with a substantial monetary help from my wife's mother, we were able to purchase our own building. I would visit my mother-in-law on a number of occasions and assured her that we would make it a priority to pay her back. I even offered to write her a promissory note to that effect.

"Son," she said lovingly, "don't you worry about doing any such thing!"

All of this was happening around Thanksgiving, and my wife and I had decided that we would not tell the members of the church about what was happening until everything was done. The pastor of the church and I devised a plan. He invited our church to attend their midweek Bible study. I told our members that we should all really try and come out in a good number to support this church and they did.

The night of the Bible study, a large group of us were there in response to the invitation. After the Bible study, the pastor asked me to come to the front. I went up, and he turned to me and said, "Pastor Hendricks, I want to hand you the keys to your new church building."

The place erupted in applause. Some of our members could hardly believe it and wondered how we were able to keep such a thing a secret from them. They were ecstatic to know that we would soon be moving into our own building.

We had agreed that the church could continue using the building until the end of the year. As soon as they moved out in early December, a team of our members moved in to clean and repaint the entire building to get it ready for services at the beginning of 2011. Not only did we have a building for our church, but it was also going to be the home of the Avenue D Boys' Choir. We had a lit sign put up on the property that read, "Family of Faith Worship Center, Home of the Avenue D Boys' Choir."

When we moved into the building for our first service, it was with mixed emotions. My wife's mother, that most wonderful lady, passed away in her sleep on New Year's Eve. We were never able to pay her back a dime from the money she lent us. But every time we gathered there for worship or for the boys to rehearse or perform, I was always conscious and thankful for that lovely little lady who gave sacrificially to help us acquire a building of our own.

She's at It Again

By the end of 2015, my life had settled into what I would call a comfortable routine. Both the church and the choir were doing well. The one main problem that had developed had to do with our personal vehicle: it was now more than fifteen years old and had begun to develop reoccurring and expensive issues. When the air-condition system went, we thought that was the last straw, so we gave it as a gift to our oldest grandchild who had just recently started driving. We were effectively without a vehicle of our own.

The temperature had gotten cooler as we approached the Christmas season that year, and so my wife and I were sitting with our garage doors opened when two vehicles drove up and parked in front of our house. Two gentlemen got out and walked toward us. One of them addressed me and asked if I was Dr. Hendricks. I said I was. He then handed me a set of keys and said that he was told to deliver the vehicle to me as a gift from a customer of his. The vehicle was a ten-year-old BMW with approximately seventy-five thousand miles. I was shocked but grateful nonetheless. I found out later that the car was a gift from a member of the church. She told me that she was so grateful for how my teaching had helped her to grow spiritually that she decided to gift me with the car as she was getting a new one for herself.

By the beginning of 2016, our new car began to develop some problems, and because our son Andrew was a mechanic, I consulted with him about getting the problems fixed. It was during one of those conversation that Andrew told me that he had to travel soon to a trial to be held in Lakeland, Florida, to support a gentleman who was being accused by his mother, Nicky, of some gravely inappropriate sexual behavior. As we talked, I became aware that the gentleman in question was someone who had attended the same high school as I had. In fact, in my final year of high school, when I was the captain of the cricket team, he had played with me on that team; his name was Errol Leslie.

As Andrew filled me in on some of the details of the impending trial, I told him that I was going to accompany him to Lakeland and see if I could also testify on behalf of Errol. Based on my prior experience with Nicky, I knew that whatever she was accusing him of was probably based on lies.

I had not seen or heard from Errol since I graduated high school in 1969, until I ran into him when he accompanied Nicky to my youngest daughter's college graduation. I remember greeting him, and his response to me was rather cold and withdrawn. I remember walking away thinking that yes, he had been "infected."

People who had been "infected" were those people that Nicky had spoken her lies to about our relationship and how and why our marriage had ended. I was to run into several of those people over the years, and I could tell that Nicky had gone out of her way to embellish and make up such nefarious lies about me that it had become obvious that she was a certifiable pathological liar. Apparently, everyone that she spoke with, she left them with some terrible stories and lies about her life with me. The interesting thing was that she would avoid people who knew us both well, as those people would know she was lying. It was the people who did not know me that were more susceptible to accepting and believing her lies. Since he had not seen or heard from me in more than forty years, Errol was an ideal candidate for her to infect with her lies.

One afternoon, not long after I saw Nicky and Errol at the graduation, I was having lunch with my wife and some friends at a Longhorn restaurant. Nicky walked into the restaurant. When she saw me, she walked right over to my table and introduced herself to my friends as Earl's ex-wife. These people had no idea up to that moment that I had been married before, and apparently, she wanted them to know. Before she left our table, she told me she needed to speak to me. She then went and sat right by the exit. As we were leaving, she got up and stood in my way and said, "I need to talk to you."

"What is it?" I asked.

She then proceeded to tell me that she was planning to get married and wanted me to do the counseling and the wedding. She made it a point to tell me that the person was someone I knew. She didn't tell me his name, but I guessed it might be Errol. I told her that I had no interest in doing that and hurried out to catch up with my wife and friends.

We were late getting to the trial in Lakeland, so when we walked in, it had already begun. I remember looking across the room and seeing the shock on Nicky's face when she saw me. Andrew took me to the table where Errol was sitting and told him that I was there to support him and would be willing to testify on his behalf. He expressed his gratitude but told me that might not be possible. It was the person representing him in the trial who explained to me that the witness list was already made up, and I could not be added to it. Now, I should make it clear here that Errol's trial was not taking place in a court of law, it was taking place in a church building.

After he graduated high school, Errol had gone on to seminary and was an ordained minister in the Methodist Church. At the time of his "trial," he had served for nearly forty years in churches in the Caribbean and the United States. About a year before this trial, Nicky had somehow gotten in touch with him, and over the course of a year, they had developed a relationship which became sexual. As the relationship grew, Nicky had begun to make demands on him, including leaving his wife to marry her. When he was not readily agreeable to that idea, she turned on him with a vengeance and wrote a handwritten eight-page letter to the leadership of the Methodist Church accusing him of, among other things, sexually abusing her, sexually abusing his own daughters, and sexually abusing the women in his church. In all, she made twenty-seven damning accusations against him in her letter. The leadership of the Methodist

Church believed her and moved to have Errol's credentials as a pastor removed so he could no longer be a minister in the church.

At the trial, the presiding judge was a retired bishop from the church, the person who was doing the prosecuting was a bishop in the church, and the person representing Errol was also a bishop from the church. I told the bishop representing Errol that I was going to go directly to the judge and ask to be allowed to testify on Errol's behalf. He told me he didn't think it would make any difference, but that he would accompany me. The bishop presiding was a little taken aback when I approached him and told him that I would like to testify on Errol's behalf. He did not ask who I was or why I wanted to testify, he just simply said no. While I was there trying to convince him to change his mind, the prosecutor walked over and told the judge that I was intimidating his chief witness, Nicky, and that he wanted me to leave. The judge called for a recess, and I went with Errol into another room to talk. As we talked, I could see the pain and distress on his face. I could see the familiar effects of what Nicky's lies, manipulation, and vengeance could do to a person.

Errol and I had not been speaking for more than five minutes when the judge and the prosecutor walked into the room and demanded that I leave the premises immediately. Not wanting to make things any the worse for Errol, I left, got in my car, and drove back home, all the while shaking my head in wonderment at another life being destroyed because the person had the misfortune of trying to forge a relationship with Nicky.

Errol was not the first guy to fall for Nicky and her convincing lies. Over the years, several other men had been roped into sexual relationships with her, and when her demanding and controlling ways proved too much, some of them had fled to get as far away from her as possible. Those that remained in close proximity to her were subjected to Nicky's relentless efforts to make their personal and professional lives as miserable as possible. And that would include going to their workplaces, homes, and churches to create embarrassing scenes, destroying their belongings, and making false accusations.

I remember one of the gentleman I met after he had moved with Nicky to live in Atlanta. I also knew him from Jamaica. In fact, he was our next-door neighbor, and I remembered him as a very gentle, courteous person. I was surprised when I was told that he and Nicky, who had been living together in New York, had now moved to Atlanta. My wife and I had gone to Atlanta to visit Nicole, and when we went to her house, Nicky and her boyfriend were there also. I somehow found myself alone with him in the front yard. Trying to make small talk, I asked him if he missed New York. He looked around, as if seeing if anyone was hearing us, and said, "Man, I can't wait to get out of here and back to New York."

As we talked further, I realized that he was very miserable with his situation. Nicky had insisted that he move with her to Atlanta. He had had to leave his job and his own children, and here he was in Atlanta with no job. I really felt sorry for the guy. It was not long afterward I was told that he packed up all his stuff, and without telling Nicky, he went back to New York without her.

About two weeks after Errol's trial, I was told that he had been found guilty on all the charges and had his credentials as a minister in the Methodist Church taken away. He was just two years away from retirement after nearly forty years of service, and now, even his pension was lost. I remember after I got back home from Lakeland, I sat down and wrote two letters, one to the judge and one to the prosecutor in which I had expressed my disgust at what I had observed at their so-called trial. But not wanting to create any further trouble for Errol, I sent him copies of the letters and asked if it was all right for me to send them. He begged me not to and so I didn't.

Several years after his trial, Errol documented his ordeal in a book called *Stolen Grace*. In it, he relayed how, at a very low point, Nicky had wormed her way into his life. After allowing himself to begin a sexual relationship with her, he realized that he was slowly creating a real spiritual dilemma for himself. He begun to express his concerns and reservations about the situation to Nicky at which point, "She played the victim game by reminding him about how horrible her ex-husband was to her and how she had had some real bad experiences with subsequent relationships."

She then began to made demands on him to divorce his wife and marry her. When he refused, she called his wife and gave her all the sordid details about their relationship, with some added disgusting allegations. These included that Errol was sexually abusing their daughters, that he didn't love her, and had told Nicky all sorts of negative things about her. When Errol's wife stood firm and refused to abandon her marriage, Nicky took it a step further and decided that if Errol wasn't going to leave his wife to marry her, she was going to destroy his life and his career. And that is what she set out to do with her eight-page handwritten letter to the church leadership. In fact, one retired Methodist pastor was quoted as saying that she told him that she was the perpetrator of what was happening to Errol. She said, "He is a wicked man. I want to destroy him."

As I read Errol's book, I noted some other interesting things that Nicky had told him about me. Of course, he had now come to realize that they were all lies. A realization that came much too late to save his career.

There was one particular story Nicky told Errol that illustrates the level she had gone to try and disparage me. Errol had apparently invited her to speak at one of his church services at which she told the story, and here, I quote directly from Errol's book, "That she had kept herself pristine and was a virgin when she married. She also told us that she and her husband, a Pentecostal pastor, had gone on a second honeymoon (after many years of marriage and having reared children, now grown) and on their return home, he shocked her by telling her he was in love with someone else and was filing for divorce." None of this was true. And as I understand it, she was telling this lie some fifteen years after the divorce.

For the twenty-five years and five months we were married, I was not a pastor. I became an ordained minister three years after the divorce and a pastor eight years after the divorce. Nicky and I had never been on a second honeymoon, and in fact, she was the one who had informed me on my return from a mission trip to Jamaica that she had been having sexual relationships with other men. But this was the extent to which she was willing to go to make up all kinds of lies to get people to sympathize with her.

I have not seen or spoken to Nicky since that day at Errol's trial, neither do I have any desire to. I have determined that I want to be as far away from that women as possible. From time to time, when my wife and I make plans to go to Atlanta to visit our grandchildren, our daughter would ask us in advance for the specific dates we will be in Atlanta. Apparently, if Nicky was going to be visiting at the same time, she did not want us crossing paths. I always appreciated her heads-up.

I bear no ill will or hatred toward Nicky; she is the mother of my children. As difficult as it was to see my first marriage end, I am keenly aware that the woman I married in my youth is not the same woman who has gone on to purposely and vengefully attempt to destroy the lives, homes, and careers of several people unfortunate enough to cross paths with her.

Sometimes, we have to go through painful extractions of people or things. But know that when we seek him, God is faithful to replace our pain with love. I have been blessed to experience both his great love and the love of my Scottie who reminds me every day that after all hope was seemingly lost, love prevails.

For Everything, There's a Season

FOR MORE THAN fourteen years, the Avenue D Boys' Choir was to provide boys, who would otherwise have been lost, with a place and an opportunity to turn their lives around. In all those years, more than three hundred boys came through the choir. There were some who came and were very talented singers, but they didn't stay too long. One thing that was constantly emphasized to the boys was that it was called a choir. There were no star performers. A boy new to the choir was required to attend at least six rehearsals before he could perform with the choir. And as far as leading a song or singing a solo, that was only for those boys who had proven themselves by their faithful attendance and consistently good grades in school.

Boys who came and right away wanted to be the featured singers soon realized that that wasn't going to happen, and they would soon leave. I don't think that in all the years of the choir, we had more than five boys who ever led a song. We never allowed solo performances. It was a choir, and that meant that everybody sang.

The years were beginning to take its toll on my wife's health. Every year from around October to February was what we called the Season. That was the time when the choir was most in demand. Despite the fact that we had volunteers helping us, it was inevitable that most things came back to her. There were a number of things that only she could handle. Teaching the boys the parts to the songs and raising funds for the choir were two of the most important.

There was a stretch of three years in a row when she ended up in the hospital and had to remain there for at least three days. Her body would just give out. Later on, we would learn that on a number of those stays she had suffered some ministrokes.

While teaching parts to a song came very easily to her, raising money for the choir was far more challenging. The choir had several buses that were used to transport the boys to and from their home for rehearsals and performances. It meant that those buses had to be insured. We needed to buy gas, new uniforms had to be purchased for the new boys joining the choir, and of course, the boys had to be fed. All this took a considerable amount of funding. And while we were getting some financial support from Children Services Council, it was not enough to meet all the needs. I would often marvel when she would turn up with a check for five thousand dollars that she had somehow persuaded someone she knew to donate to the choir.

In late 2017, we had to go to England for the funeral of one of my sisters. While there, my wife became very ill. She was still not fully recovered when we return to the States. The night, we got back and had gone to bed when at about one o'clock in the morning, she suddenly sat up in the bed gasping for air. I tried patting her on her back to see if that would help, but it didn't. I hurried to the phone to call 911, but nobody answered. I had no alternative but to plead the blood of Jesus over her as I quickly got dressed to rush her to the hospital. Our granddaughter, hearing the commotion, got up and came to our room to find out what was happening. As I got ready to go out the door, the phone rang. It was the 911 dispatcher calling back. I hung up the phone and, with my wife still having some difficulty breathing, rushed her to the hospital.

At the hospital, the doctors were unable to say definitively what the problem was. They felt that she probably had some sort of viral infection, but they weren't certain. We left the hospital with her breathing returning to normal, but that very night, the same thing happened again, and again I had to rush her back to the hospital. This time, the doctors did a number of tests, but still couldn't determine what the problem was, and after keeping her for a day, they sent her home.

For the next four months, my wife was unable to function in any capacity whatsoever. She couldn't walk, she spoke at barely a whisper, and she was weak with a fever. Since the doctors couldn't find anything specifically wrong with her, I did my best to take care of her and made sure she was as comfortable as possible. It was only after the COVID-19 pandemic began that we were able to identify her symptoms as being exactly like those of someone with COVID-19.

After about four months, she slowly began to get her strength back and was able to return to some sort of normalcy. But she was never the same again. She kept getting sick on a regular basis, and finally, I told her that maybe it was time for her to give up the choir since it was taking too much of a toll on her health. She was reluctant to do so. The choir was her baby. She had built it and watched as a young man after young man came through that choir with their lives transformed. She didn't just want to see it end. So she tried finding someone to take over the choir in her place. She could find no one, and so in September of 2018, nine months after she first became gravely ill, she reluctantly closed down the choir for good.

A lot of people were sorry to see the end of the choir. The fourteen years that it was in existence was the longest any locally run organization like it had existed. We would have loved to see someone take it over and move forward with it, but try as we may, we could not find anyone with the same passion and desire to do so. My wife's health had to be protected at all costs as far as I was concerned, and to do so meant that she had to give up the choir, and that was what she did.

That's Enough

AFTER I GRADUATED with my doctoral degree in 1997, I immediately began the process to be certified to become an administrator in the school system. This included taking more graduate-level courses as well as successfully completing the Florida Educational Leadership Exam (FELE).

The FELE is an eight-hour exam that tests you in the broad areas of leadership in education including school management, school communication, and school operations. Under these broad headings were individual areas like leadership, personnel, law, technology, finance, and curriculum. It was such an intense exam that if you pass just one of the three broad areas, you can bank it while you take the others over. You have to be successful in all three areas in order to pass the FELE. I passed the entire exam in just one sitting.

By the time I received my doctorate, I had been teaching in a public school in St. Lucie County for six years. During that time, I received rave reviews from my principals for my exceptional abilities in the classroom. On the instrument used for my annual evaluation, it was not unusual for the word "Exceptional" to be regularly used to describe my abilities in such areas as knowledge of the subject matter, presentation of subject matter, communication: verbal and nonverbal, and management of student conduct.

One of my principals, Mrs. Gerri McPherson wrote this: "Dr. Earl Hendricks is always distinguished and appropriate in his professional dress, mannerisms, and dealing with colleagues. He is exemplary in assuming responsibility for his own professional development. Dr. Hendricks manifests an exemplary outlook and exhibits a conscientious concern. His literate and scholastic foundation is readily recognizable and he manifests complete authority over the subject matter."

It was because of evaluations like those, plus what I had done to be certified by the State of Florida in Educational Leadership, that I began applying for administrative positions in the school system. And for three years, I did not receive even one invitation for an interview. I was beginning to wonder why when an assistant superintendent, who had just taken up a new position with a school district in another county, stopped by my classroom one day to speak with me.

"You are not being considered for any leadership position in the county," he said, "because they have blackballed you."

He explained that because of the time I had lost my temper in the classroom and another time when a white parent got in my face and I stood up and told him, "Bring it on," the personnel office had put a red flag in my file. They considered those two incidents to be unprofessional conduct. He was only telling me, he said, because he was on his way out, and he thought I ought to know. It clarified a lot of things for me. Looking back, I think that was part of the reasons why I decided to accept the position of headmaster of Munro College in Jamaica. I was angry about what they were doing to me, and I needed to get as far away from these people far as I could.

I stayed in Jamaica for two and a half years before I returned and began teaching again in the same school district. After eighteen months in the classroom and continuing to receive exceptional annual evaluations, I decided to try again for an administrative position. There was an opening for a vice principal at one of the high schools, and I applied. Having had more than two years' experience as a principal, I thought that maybe they would look more favorable on my application now after so many years had passed. To my surprise, not only was I interviewed, but I was offered the job as well.

A few days after being chosen for the position, I received a phone call that the Director of Personnel at the District Office wanted to see me. When I went to see her, she reminded me of both incidents that had resulted in me being blackballed and told me that now that I was an assistant principal, such behavior must never be repeated. I wasn't about to argue with her about anything, so I assured her it would not and I left.

I served as an assistant principal for three years, one year in a high school and two years in a middle school. During that time, I participated in the Principal Internship Program that was designed to prepare assistant principals to become principals in the county. At the end of the three years, of all the people who participated with me in the program, I was the only one that was recommended to be certified as a principal. It was also after those three years that the school district decided that I should return to the classroom to be a regular teacher again. I was confused.

Why would they recommend me to be certified to become a principal and then send me back to the classroom? When I spoke to my principal about it, she told me that it had become obvious to her that my passion was no longer for teaching, and she would suggest that I concentrate on my work with the Avenue D Boys Choir and as the pastor of Family of Faith Worship Center.

At the time, I was not in agreement with her assessment, but later, I came to realize how correct she was. After being back in the classroom for a little while, I realized that I no longer had the desire or the passion for dealing with kids. My wife and my grandson told me they could see how frustrated I was becoming and was hoping I would quit. They said that every weekend I came home, I would be relaxed and at ease until the Sunday afternoon before I had to return to school the following morning, and they could see how tense and withdrawn I would become.

It was in the middle of the 2009–2010 school year when I finally decided that I had had enough, and I submitted my resignation to the principal. She begged me to reconsider or to at least stay until the end of the school year. But I told her I didn't want to do that, and so when school broke for the Christmas holidays in December 2009, I went home and never went back.

Time to Give This Up Too

THE CHURCH AND the boys' choir ran parallel to each other for nearly fourteen years. The boys' choir began in March of 2004, and the church started in April of the same year. For the first twenty-two months, we were part of Pastor Brown's church, and then beginning in March of 2007, it became Family of Faith Worship Center.

We formed the new church as a nonaffiliated, nondenominational, full-gospel church. We were approached on numerous occasions to become part of some other organized groups, but we always declined. I had seen what that could lead to, and I didn't want to go through that again.

We moved into our own building in January 2011 and having our own building quickly resulted in a rapid growth in our membership. I remember one Sunday morning when we offered the right hand of fellowship to twenty-five new members. The church would continue to grow, but never at that pace. At its height, the church had over three hundred members.

The thing that I was particularly happy to see was the number of white folks who had become members. I have always felt that it was far better for believers of all races to worship together. The sad thing is that the eleven o'clock hour on a Sunday morning in America is still the most segregated time of the week. And that is the time when people who claim to believe in the same Savior choose to worship only with people of their own race rather than choosing to join together with all others to worship the Lord. It is truly a sad, sad reflection on the body of Christ.

After my wife got sick on her visit to England, it wasn't until about April of 2018 before she was well enough to try and get back to doing what she normally does. It soon became obvious that wasn't going to happen. We thought that by giving up the choir and only having to help with the church would be good for her.

For a while we were doing fine, but from time to time, it became obvious that that too was becoming too much for her as well. I didn't know it at the time, but she had begun praying earnestly for the Lord to deliver (her? Us?) from that responsibility as well. I soon began thinking that maybe we should give the church to someone else so she would no longer have that pressure to deal with. There was one major problem.

We had been able to pay down our mortgage on the building to where we now owed only about two hundred thousand dollars. The bank had insisted that my wife and I were the ones personally responsible for the payment of the mortgage. Over the years, we had never had to take money directly out of our pockets to make payments, but each year, we were the ones giving nearly a quarter of the total amount that the church received each year. We could think of no one that we could turn the church over to who we could be confident that we wouldn't still have to carry the burden of that mortgage payment. We began to look for ways to raise all the money to pay off the mortgage, after which we felt we would be free of any concerns if we turn the church over to someone else. We were never able to find the necessary funds to do so.

About a year after we gave up the boys' choir, my wife was still struggling with her health. Finding a way to give up being pastors became even more urgent. It was then that she suggested that we go and speak to two friends of ours, a husband and wife, who were pastoring a church out of their home.

We wanted to find out if they would be interested in taking over the mortgage on the building and having it for their church. They were very enthusiastic about the idea, but when we went to the bank, they threw cold water on the idea. The only way they could do that, according to the bank, was if they applied for a loan to pay off the old mortgage and put the church and the mortgage in their name. That was fine with us since that meant that we wouldn't be in any way responsible for the mortgage going forward.

Once again, my wife and I made certain that we had all the necessary arrangements in place before we told anyone. After the arrangements were finalized, we called a meeting of our leadership and explained to them what we were planning to do. They were very supportive, especially in light of the effect everything was having on my wife's health. We then had a members' meeting to explain what was happening. They too were very understanding and supportive. And so, on Sunday, May 5, 2019, my wife and I had our last day as the pastors of Family of Faith Worship Center. It had been fifteen years since we first met as a church and just over eight years since we had been in our own building.

Family of Faith Worship Center ceased to exist that day, and Yahweh Hands-On Ministry became the new owners of the building. One thing we were really pleased to see was that most of the people, who had been part of Family of Faith, chose to stay and become a part of Yahweh Hands-On Ministry.

Epilogue

ONE OF THE immediate concerns my wife and I had after we stepped down as pastors was where we would be attending church in the future. We felt that staying at Yahweh would probably not be a good idea since we wanted the new pastor to establish himself in his new building without any confusion about leadership. Fortunately for us, the Lord showed us where we should fellowship.

About a month before we stepped down, we had gone to see the movie *Breakthrough* with our daughter and her husband. As we were leaving the theater after the movie, I was holding the door open so they could walk through. Right behind them was a group of about eight people, and so I continued holding the door open for them to come through as well. The last person through was an elderly gentleman who, as he came through the door, said to me, "You must be a deacon in a church?"

"Actually, I am a pastor," I said.

"I can see you have a servant's heart," he said.

As we spoke further, he informed me that he was a retired pastor himself. His name was Bill Jerrils. It just so happened that his group and our family were also going to the same restaurant for lunch. And when we sat down, they were seated just across the way from us. After lunch, as we were preparing to leave, I asked him where he worshipped. He said Pathway. So when we stepped down as pastors, we immediately thought that we would go and visit this gentleman's church.

It has been over three years since we first visited Pathway. We have found it to be a great teaching and praying church, and so we have become active members there. It was Bill Jerrils's sweet Christlike disposition that caused us to come to visit. But it is without doubt, the Bible-based teachings and the loving and friendly people are why we have remained.

A Final Word

WHEN I BEGAN writing this book, I had no idea how long it would take or even if I would have much to say. As it turned out, completing it became an obsession with me. There were times when my wife had to actually come to remind me to get up from the computer and take a rest. I was also really surprised at the number of things I was able to remember and the details with which I was able to recall them. As much as possible, I have tried to be as accurate as I could with quotations.

One of my reasons for writing this book was to use it as an avenue to express my heartfelt appreciation for those people who have blessed my life in so many ways. There are people like the Meads and my first foster parents, who have all played invaluable roles in helping me to be the person I have become.

Mrs. Marie Joseph or Aunt Mar—we called her Mother—was the first person who instilled in me the importance of an education. She was a woman who had very little education herself, yet she recognized its importance and insisted that we go to school. I am so glad she was not like most people living in the country parts of Jamaica at the time. While many of them might have felt that education was important, they just didn't have the opportunity or resources to encourage their children to go on to high school, much less college.

Mr. and Mrs. Mead are true giants to me in that they have opened their home and their lives to me could only have come from hearts that loved the Lord with a passion. It was at Mrs. Mead's insistence that I went to college and became a teacher.

And then there is my wife, Scottie. She is without a doubt the most exceptional person I have ever met. Her humility, her giftedness, and her dedication to whatever she does has been such an example to me. She is the one who taught me to love again and to trust again. My life would be absolutely nothing without her. The world is a better place because she lives in it.

And then there is he who is, without doubt, the most definitive of all difference makers, the Lord Jesus Christ. No one has had the impact on my life that the Lord Jesus has. He has transformed my very life completely by his grace. He has truly taken me out of darkness into his marvelous light.

I remember when I first began to understand that it was all by his grace that it was almost unbelievable to me. And yet it is all true. He loved me even when I felt unlovable. He was with me even at those times when I felt most alone. There is a verse in Psalms 27:10 that proved the truth of God's faithfulness to me over the years. It says, "Even if my father and mother abandon me, the Lord will hold me close."

And recently, I heard the chorus to a song that fully expresses my heart's attitude and response to the Lord: "All my life, you have been faithful. All my life, you have been so, so good. So with every breath that I am able, I will sing of the goodness of God."

That truly expresses how I feel. I will never cease to give him thanks and praise for his goodness to me. The Lord Jesus Christ, there is none like him to me.

And when we receive him as our Savior, it is then that the righteousness that is his, he gives to us as his gift of salvation. And when you receive that gift, you will want to live each day filled with gratitude. And a life filled with gratitude to God is a life lived in daily victory over any circumstance and situation that life throws at you.

And there are so many other people that I could mention who have made invaluable contributions to my life. Whether they have passed on or are still with us, I just want to say a big "thank you very much" and a big "God bless you."

Now, it was never my intention to cast blame or aspersions on anyone for any of the negative things that happened in my life. In a way, I am glad that things happened to me the way they did. If those things hadn't happened the way they did, I am sure I wouldn't be where I am today, and I certainly wouldn't be the person I am.

I believe that each situation helped to make me a better man, a better father, and certainly a much better husband to my Scottie. I have often told her that the only way I could possibly have had the opportunity to meet her was if all the things in my life happened exactly the way they did. It's definitely the case of "All things work together for good…"

So in spite of all the things that have happened to me, I am still very grateful for the life that God has allowed me to live *despite it all!*

And so there you have it. I'm done. I've written a book.

About the Author

AUTHOR DR. EARL W. Hendricks lives with his family in Florida. He is originally from the island of Jamaica. He has earned degrees from Mercy College and Long Island University in New York and Nova Southeastern University in Florida.

He is a retired educator and pastor who now enjoys his full-time position as husband, father, and grandfather. When he is not preparing sermons or watching sports, he is traveling the world with his wife of twenty-five years. He and his wife, Mary, are the parents of eight children and fourteen grandchildren who are the focus of their energy.

In *A Life Lived, Despite It All,* Dr. Hendricks shares his story of abandonment, loss, and perseverance, inviting us into a life well lived. His debut book highlights how the grace of God can help us overcome life's hurts and disappointments and propel us forward to fulfill God's purpose and plan, despite it all.

Milton Keynes UK
Ingram Content Group UK Ltd.
UKHW010638120124
435917UK00001B/114

9 798890 435378